Twilight of the Long-ball Gods

Dispatches from the
Disappearing Heart of Baseball

JOHN SCHULIAN

University of Nebraska Press, Lincoln and London

Acknowledgments for the
use of previously pub-
lished material appear on
pages 183–84, which con-
stitute an extension of the
copyright page.

Manufactured in the
United States of America
∞

Library of Congress Cata-
loging-in-Publication
Data
Schulian, John, 1945– twilight of the long-ball gods:
dispatches from the disappearing heart of baseball /
John Schulian.   p.   cm.
Includes bibliographical
references. ISBN 0-8032-
9327-5 (pbk.: alk. paper)
1. Minor league baseball –
United States. 2. Baseball
players – United States. I.
Title. GV875.A1S38 2005
796.357'64'0973–dc22
2004021035
Set in Minion by Bob
Reitz. Designed by Dika
Eckersley. Printed by
Edwards Brothers, Inc.

In memory of Eliot Wald

Contents

Introduction

I grew up reading the *Sporting News* from back to front, like a grizzled shortstop who couldn't climb higher than Pocatello yet never stopped loving the idea that somebody was paying him to play baseball, slave wages or no. The obvious explanation for such a curious boyhood habit was that I lived in Los Angeles in the days before the Dodgers, when the Pacific Coast League was as good as we got. (And damn good it was, incidentally.) The *Sporting News'* back pages were, at least in the mid-'50s, a repository for dispatches from the game's far reaches, the minor leagues, the bushes. From Class D, which no longer exists, to the Open Classification Coast League, which considered itself better than merely Triple A, there were standings, statistics, and ragged little stories about tank-town heroes. Like my friends, I worshipped at the shrines of Mays and Mantle, Williams, Musial, and Robinson, but I always had this secret place where the *Sporting News* would take me and nobody else.

Amid one-inch ads for baseball schools in the Ozarks, Fran Boniar was batting over .400 for the Reno Silver Sox, Bob Lennon was wearing out the short porch in right field at Nashville's Sulfur Dell, and ancient Clarence "Hooks" Iott was throwing junk down in St. Pete. Anything I couldn't find out about them and their kind, I imagined, as if life really were a novel by John R. Tunis.

My introduction to the unvarnished but no less intriguing truth about the minors came one rainy Saturday morning when I was twelve. Fresh from the barbershop, I pedaled my bike over to the newsstand where I did my best reading and picked up *True* magazine's *1957 Baseball Annual*. At the heart of it, physically and spiritually, lay one of W. C. Heinz's masterpieces, "The Rocky Road of Pistol Pete." Here was the story of Pete Reiser, the victim of too many collisions with too many outfield walls when he played for the Dodgers, managing in Kokomo, baseball's bottom rung, with a bum heart and a broken-down Chevy. Hardly standard fare for a kid still full of big-league dreams, and yet there was no denying the ache and the courage that Heinz captured in his memorably understated way.

I felt it then, I feel it now, and I can't help thinking that the seed for this book was planted in that first reading. One vintage piece of journalism galvanized the bittersweet poetry I had intuited in the game's distant outposts. There were stories worth telling in the vagabonds who dwelled out there, lost, forgotten, overlooked. So it is that I come to you with some of my own as the era that spawned them is going, going, gone.

On and off for the past thirty years, I've been able to find editors – at *Sports Illustrated*, GQ, the *Chicago Daily News*, the *Chicago Sun-Times*, the *Philadelphia Daily News*, *Philadelphia* magazine, the original *Inside Sports*, the *National* and, inevitably, the *Sporting News* – who would let me indulge my passion for baseball's shadow world. Most of my subjects were culled from minor leagues and mining towns, Negro leagues and sandlots. Those few stories that feature names you recognize – Babe Ruth, Bill Veeck, Studs Terkel – are included because they speak to the humanity that big money, modern marketing, and a changing culture have inexorably leeched out of baseball. But please don't look at this collection as an assault on the state of the game now that Wrigley Field has lights and Barry Bonds has hit seventy-three home runs in a season. The past was hardly better in every way, and all you need for proof is the fact that Josh Gibson and Jimmie Crutchfield, men I wrote about proudly, *black* men, never had a chance to play in the big leagues.

What they created in exile, however, was a thing of beauty and passion. They were denied fame, money, even sandwiches at a roadside stand, but never the joy that came with playing the game that was their lifeblood. And that same indomitable quality runs through all the other subjects I have gathered here, men who, to borrow a line from a Tom Waits song, "lived on nothin' but dreams and train smoke." No matter how many times baseball broke their hearts, they kept coming back for more. Most were marooned in the splintered bush league firetraps of yore. But even one who wasn't, a wandering slugger named Russ Morman, learned that Durham's hip retro ballpark offered no salvation from the unanswered prayers that are as old as baseball itself.

I liked Morman as much as anybody I have written about, and I admired him even more. It is one thing, after all, to be Alex Rodriguez or Roger Clemens – not an easy thing, either, since greatness brings with it unfathomable burdens – and yet Rodriguez and Clemens never carried the weight that Morman did. He was one step shy of an enduring big league career, probably less than that, and there he would stay, facing the truth with a dignity that made him more of a man than better players would ever be.

Underdogs always appeal to writers, of course, and losers have historically been more open to inspection and introspection than winners, but I was drawn to them before I knew that's what they were. In a youth that was split between minor-league Los Angeles and Salt Lake City, I cared not a whit that Paul Pettit, Spook Jacobs and Sam Miley, to name just a few, were fated to labor in obscurity for as long as they played. They were the heroes who mattered most to me because I could see them with my own eyes. And I had friends who operated on the same principle. The one who leaps to mind is a second baseman who came home from a summer of pro ball in North Carolina to proudly report that he had played against Chuck Weatherspoon. The very same Chuck Weatherspoon he had watched wallop home runs for the Missoula Mustangs years before. It was a sight I'd never beheld, but I still knew who Weatherspoon was. I'd read about him in the *Sporting News*.

Though I've always been able to rhapsodize endlessly about those days, there was a time when I stopped loving baseball. It happened in the mid-'80s, after I'd seen too much of it and every other sport, dealt with too many new-breed athletes, soaked up a lifetime supply of press-box cynicism, and probably read too much of my own prose. I fled the *Philadelphia Daily News* and headed for Hollywood, an unusual choice for rebirth of any kind but the only place I could think of where it looked like I still might be able to make a living as a writer.

All these years later, I've survived as much as anyone working in TV does. I've had good times writing for *Miami Vice*, *Wiseguy*, *Midnight Caller*, *Hercules*, and *JAG*, and, thanks to a confluence of luck and other people's talent, I can call myself the co-creator of *Xena: Warrior Princess*. But it's still a feast or famine business, and the first time I experienced famine, I groped for a way to hold my ground. Then it came to me: I would write for *Sports Illustrated* about Los Angeles when I was a kid and how two Coast League teams fought for my heart and the city's.

Doing that story proved to be a tonic that more than rekindled my feelings for baseball, with its myriad games on cable and the trips to Dodger Stadium that are the absolute best thing about summer evenings in L.A. The story started me thinking about the players I had loved first and best, the ones whose fame rarely went beyond the city limits of Roswell or Wisconsin Rapids. Time had left them behind, and age was catching up with them. I realized it when I saw Roger Bowman, an old Hollywood Star left-hander, a year after I'd interviewed him for my *SI* piece. He had been so full of life, playing tennis daily, packing away steak dinners that would have foundered men half his age, and now his step was reduced to a shuffle. Another year and he would be dead.

I hope Roger Bowman read what I wrote before he breathed his last. I wanted him to know that he mattered in a way that doesn't seem possible when your career is stamped *minor league*. And I want you to know the same about him and everybody like him, all the dreamers, bust-outs, and hard-luck cases. I think of them now, riding a train headed around a bend and out of sight forever. I hear that lonesome whistle blow, and I ask you to take a moment and listen to it too.

1

Of Stars and Angels

These are the memories that make me a kid again, these memories of a Los Angeles that I can scarcely believe existed and of two Pacific Coast League teams not so much forgotten as overwhelmed by the city's ceaseless charge into the future.

So let me take you back to the early '50s and a Friday night at Gilmore Field, home of the Hollywood Stars. You could always see big names there – Spencer Tracy, Barbara Stanwyck and that crowd – and my parents may well have been looking for them. But I wasn't, because a Star pitcher named Red Munger had caught me staring at him and his enormous chaw of tobacco. Maybe we had box seats, although I can't ever recall our being in that economic bracket, or maybe my head of corn-silk hair stood out like a beacon in the twilight. Time turns so many things hazy, but I do know this: Red Munger grinned and said, "Hiya, Whitey." It was the first time a baseball player ever spoke to me.

Thirty years later, long past being thrilled by conversations with ballplayers, long past even expecting them, I was a Chicago sports columnist covering the dying quiver of a pennant race, but my mind was on old fascinations. I thought of Carlos Bernier, the Star left fielder who loved arguing with umpires as much as he did stealing bases, and of Johnny Lindell, the dead-armed ex-Yankee outfielder who became a knuckleball pitcher in Hollywood. Mostly I thought of Steve Bilko, who hit so many home runs for the PCL's Los Angeles Angels that I almost gave up on the Stars.

The floodgates of memory had opened, and all because Gene Mauch was in town.

He had been the Angels' second baseman back then, and now, in 1982, he had come to old Comiskey Park as the manager of another band of Angels, the American Leaguers from California. They were in the process of wrapping up a division championship, yet Mauch still labored under the shadow of past failures and a sense that his future would be just as bleak. He never expected anyone to ask about the Coast League and the best days he ever had as a player. When I did, his match stopped short of his cigarette, and his steely gaze softened.

"Where the hell did you come from?" Mauch asked.

He was almost smiling.

§ I come from the same place Gene Mauch does, a Los Angeles still golden with promise and perfumed by eucalyptus and citrus trees. It is where I was born; it is where Mauch's father migrated when there were no more oil wells to drill in Kansas. As a kid, I lived in the same neighborhood as Mauch, and I remember the other ballplayers who called Inglewood home, too: George Metkovich, Peanuts Lowrey, and even the National League's 1952 Most Valuable Player, Hank Sauer. Like so many things viewed in retrospect, that seems a better time. At the very least, it was simpler.

You never traveled by freeway then unless you were going to Pasadena, birthplace of those concrete snakes. There were buses; there were the venerable Red Line streetcars; there were the old coupes that you always wished could fly when they were winding you over Laurel Canyon or Beverly Glen into the San Fernando Valley. And then there were the bikes that Irv Noren and his buddy Norm Hallajian rode to see the Angels play in Wrigley Field, the double-decked replica of its Chicago namesake. This is the same Irv Noren who grew up to give the Stars an MVP season in 1949 and then patrolled the outfield for the Washington Senators and the New York Yankees. But in the late '30s he was a transplant from upstate New York, a baker's son who prayed he was seeing his destiny every Saturday when he and Norm pedaled from their Pasadena homes down through Eagle Rock and Highland Park, past downtown Los

Angeles, and on to Wrigley, at 42nd and Avalon, just southeast of the Coliseum.

"We'd park right in front of the stadium," Noren says, "just lean our bikes against the wall and go in with the Knothole Gang. Wouldn't even lock 'em."

And when the game was over, the bikes were always there.

By the '50s, when I came along, the innocence was beginning to fade. Friends who rode the bus to Wrigley said neighborhood kids roughed them up, but Los Angeles, even with its postwar population soaring past two million, was still a long way from having calluses on its soul. Though Raymond Chandler's Philip Marlowe mused that the city's streets were "lost and beaten and full of emptiness," I remember that they all seemed to lead to the pony ride at Beverly and La Cienega, where the Beverly Center now teems with upscale shoppers. What crime I recall – show-biz bloodlettings, pachuco gang fights in East L.A. – was splashed across the front page of William Randolph Hearst's afternoon *Herald Express*, 65 copies of which I faithfully delivered Monday through Saturday. The only gangster I was aware of was Mickey Cohen, who, as a favor to the *Herald*'s headline-hungry city editor, stole Lana Turner's love letters to the hood her teenage daughter stabbed to death. Mickey Cohen rooted for the Stars.

George Raft rooted for them too, and both he and Cohen were tight with Bugsy Siegel, so I can only assume that Bugsy made it to Gilmore Field before his untimely demise. Lord knows every other celebrity did. If Gary Cooper, Rosemary Clooney, and Milton Berle weren't in the stands, Bing Crosby, Cecil B. DeMille, and Burns and Allen were. Some of the big names held stock in the Stars, a tribute to the sway of the team's dapper owner, Bob Cobb, president of the Brown Derby and inventor of the Cobb salad.

But the thespian who made the biggest impact was Jayne Mansfield. When sweet Jayne high-heeled out of the dugout as Miss Hollywood Stars, there was an awe-inspired silence at the way her chest defied gravity. As the males in the crowd began roaring lustily, skipper Clyde King, as courtly and God-fearing a southern gentleman as ever graced the game, whispered, "Goodness gracious."

Before Los Angeles had any Dodgers or big league Angels, any Lakers or Raiders or Clippers or Kings, you had to go a long way to beat La Mansfield's act. Only the Rams could do it, luring 100,000 paying customers into the Coliseum each Sunday, and yet, as late as 1949, the Stars remained the toughest ticket in town. But the town, if you judged by its tastes, was still shamelessly small-time. Forget all the hoorah about college football at Southern Cal and UCLA. Forget all the cigar smoke that got blown about the club fights at the Olympic Auditorium and Hollywood American Legion Stadium and the title fights at Wrigley and Gilmore Fields. The Los Angeles I choose to remember devoted far more passion to professional wrestling, both live and televised, from the Olympic, from Legion Stadium, from South Gate, from Ocean Park Arena (with none other than Steve Allen at the ringside mike). So great was L.A.'s hunger for these sweaty morality plays that Channel 11 had to pipe even more of them in from Las Vegas. How fitting for a city where a good Sunday afternoon of TV sports meant watching semipro football and the Jalopy Derby from Culver City Stadium.

When I think back to all that raw exuberance and unbridled tackiness, it seems the Coast League gave L.A. sports a rare touch of . . . well, *dignity* isn't the word, not with the shorts the Stars insisted on wearing in the '50s and the call-the-cops brawls they had with the Angels. But *normality*, maybe, because no matter how outrageous the two teams got, they still played baseball; they still did something connected to the rest of the country and not confined to Planet California.

Consider Gus Zernial, the slugging outfielder revered as Ozark Ike by Hollywood fans in '47 and '48. He burst on the scene at the same time as wrestling's flamboyant Gorgeous George, but did he peroxide his hair and throw gold-plated bobby pins to his admirers? No, sir, Gus went out and hit 40 homers in his second season as a Star, the way any regular guy would if he had a quick bat and a ton of muscles. And believe me, these minor league heroes were regular guys. They lived among us, they worked among us. My dad bought a '56 Chevy from Lou Stringer, a nifty second baseman for both Los Angeles and Hollywood, and he could just as easily have made the deal with Eddie Malone, who toiled for each team as an iron-man catcher. If my parents had needed any upholstering done, they could have gone to Roger Bowman, the Star left-hander who had a shop in Santa Monica. And we could always roll a few lines at Irv Noren's bowling alley.

No one remembered the intimacy of the times and the town better than Chuck Connors, who didn't realize he was only pausing in the Angels' lineup on his way to a place in television history as *The Rifleman*. When the Chicago Cubs farmed him to L.A. in 1951, Connors bought a tract house in Reseda, never thinking how long a drive it was to that Valley outpost in those pre-101 freeway days. He found out the first time he had to make the 25-mile haul across the Cahuenga Pass after a Saturday night game, with a Sunday afternoon doubleheader just hours away. It looked like Connors had a lot of sleepless weekends ahead until a family that lived across the street from Wrigley Field approached him.

"I'd known them for a while," he told me shortly before his death last year. "I'd gotten them signed baseballs, some gloves, things like that." Now they were offering to return the favor by putting Connors up on Saturday nights. He accepted instantly. "I'd sleep in their extra bedroom," Connors said, "and Sunday morning I'd eat breakfast with them." He was a first baseman from Brooklyn who happened to be white, they were Angel fans who happened to be black, and this was a Los Angeles that we would never see again.

§ The big man was Bilko, and I'm talking about more than the excess poundage that inspired a *Los Angeles Times* headline saying "Not Even Mrs. Bilko Knows His Weight." I'm talking about the feats that enabled Stout Steve, the Slugging Seraph, to block out the big league sun for my generation of L.A. kids.

Thirty-seven home runs in '55, 55 in '56, 56 in '57 – who needed Mays or Mantle, Williams or Musial, when we had Bilko making that kind of noise? True, he had washed out of the majors after a 21-homer season with the St. Louis Cardinals in 1953, and there was no denying that the Coast League pitchers he hit best were mediocrities. But it was far more important that he wasn't some remote god who never deigned to come closer to Los Angeles than the western bank of the Mississippi. You could watch Bilko bash another one out of Wrigley Field and get a moon-faced grin afterward when you shoved your scorecard at him for an autograph.

Little did I know that he was upholding a long and honorable tradition. Almost since the Coast League had hit town in 1903, there had been one charismatic galoot or another on hand to make L.A. forget what it was and he wasn't. The most enduring of them all was Jigger Statz, who would have been memorable on the strength of his name alone if he hadn't brought so much more to the Angels. For 18 years, the longest run any player ever had with a single minor league team, Jigger roamed center field wearing a glove he had carved the palm out of – all the better for feeling the ball, you understand – and making catches that still had native son Duke Snider in awe when he was vying with Mays and Mantle for the kingship of New York. "The writers would ask Duke who the best center fielder he ever saw was," Noren recalls, "and Duke would always say Jigger Statz."

Statz was just a little rascal, not quite 5-foot-8; he couldn't have weighed more than 150 pounds with rocks in his pockets, but he was Bilko's match when it came to casting shadows. He stole as many as 61 bases in a season, batted as high as .360, and Gene Mauch remembers skipping school in 1942, Statz's farewell campaign, to watch him hit two homers on opening day. ("Only two he hit all year," Mauch says.) And yet, for all of that, there was something missing, something that kept Statz from sticking with the Cubs and the Brooklyn Dodgers. Los Angeles was his safety net.

Bilko knew the feeling. So did most of the other Stars and Angels I worshipped as a kid. For every Bill Mazeroski or Dale Long, every Noren or Zernial who blew through town on his way to the big show, there were dozens of others who couldn't survive in that rarefied 16-team atmosphere. But I didn't care that Frank Kelleher hadn't cut it in Cincinnati's outfield; he was the heart of the Stars, an amiable lug who hit 226 homers in 10 seasons and got to see his beloved number 7 retired. Nor did it matter to me that the New York Giants had found Roger Bowman wanting; it was more important that the last of his 22 wins in 1954 was a perfect game that tied Hollywood with the original San Diego Padres for first place.

"We were journeymen, I was well aware of that," Bowman says. "But I kept playing for the simple reason that this was what I did best and what I loved best. When I quit, it was going to be forever. So I told myself that until that happened, I was going to suck the marrow right out of the game."

In every other town in the Coast League, tough, proud men echoed that sentiment with bats, balls, and, more than occasionally, fists. Some of them you've probably never heard of – Joe Brovia in Portland, Earl Rapp in Oakland and San Diego. But others had names that still ring a bell. Ernie Lombardi, a Hall of Fame career in the National League behind him, caught for Casey Stengel's Oakland Oaks until he was in his forties. Joe Gordon, the old Yankee second baseman, hit 43 homers as the Sacramento Solons' playing manager in 1951, and two years later, Bob Dillinger, owner of a .306 career average in the majors, rang up a league-leading .366 for the Solons. And how about Bob Elliott, whose two home runs led San Diego past the Stars in their one-game '54 pennant playoff? Seven years earlier, Elliott had been the toast of the Boston Braves and the MVP in the National League. Add those men to the Angels and the Stars and you have far more than a league that fulfilled its duty when it spawned Joe DiMaggio and Ted Williams. You have the best minor league ever.

"The best by far," says former Hollywood right-hander Ben Wade, who studied the Triple A competition when he played in the International League and the American Association. The Coast League of Wade's era wound up with five of its towns in the majors – Los Angeles, San Francisco, Oakland, San Diego, and Seattle. But long before then, its teams were traveling in big league fashion. Oh, there were still trains – Cece Carlucci, the old umpire, is unashamedly poetic when he talks about pulling into Seattle on the Great Northern – but by the mid-'50s airplanes were the thing. "Three-hundred-mile-an-hour Convairs," Bowman says. "Boy, that was hot stuff." And wherever the planes landed was somewhere the players didn't mind being, which was good because they hit each town for a week at a time. They would play single games Tuesday through Saturday and a doubleheader on Sunday, the second game being what sportswriters unfailingly referred to as "the abbreviated seven-inning nightcap."

It may have been the most civilized existence baseball has ever seen, and payday made it better yet. "I came from the big leagues and got a pay raise," Chuck Stevens says. Maybe the 1949 Stars were in better shape to pay this slick-fielding, spray-hitting first baseman than the St. Louis Browns had been; after all, Hollywood's pennant winners drew nearly 600,000 fans. But you hear the same story again and again from former Stars and Angels, which suggests that money preoccupied ballplayers even when they made seven grand a year.

Not that seven grand was the ceiling. "I'll bet Frank Kelleher pulled down 15, maybe even 17 thousand dollars," Noren says. And there have always been stories that Bilko took a pay cut when Cincinnati summoned him back to the bigs in 1958.

Of course I was no more aware of that than I was of the fact that the Stars' and Angels' insistence on televising every home game was eating their attendance alive. All I knew was that TV made it that much easier to watch baseball played by men toughened by the Depression and World War II, men who threw to the right base, balked at the idea of batting helmets, and wouldn't let Zernial wear gold shoelaces when he made his debut in a Hollywood uniform. The shoelaces, I hasten to point out, weren't Zernial's idea; they were on the only pair of spikes he could find as he hurried to join the Stars in time for opening day. Fair enough, but his new teammates still made Zernial give the laces a coat of black shoe polish. If anyone wanted to be colorful, he had to do it on terms the veterans understood. He could throw ground beef to the boo-birds in San

Francisco, the way Chuck Connors did. Or he could get back at the umpires the way Hollywood manager Bobby Bragan did when they didn't enforce the curfew in his own ballpark: the next night Bragan sent a coach to home plate with watches up and down his arm and an alarm clock around his neck.

But what they did most of all in Los Angeles, Hollywood, and the rest of the Coast League was play baseball. And no minor leaguers ever played it better than the 1956 Angels. Here was a powerhouse to make me forget about Hollywood's pennant winners of '49, '52, and '53. These Angels won 107 games, 16 more than second-place Seattle. They batted .297 as a team and had six players with 20 or more homers, including the Punch-and-Judy Mauch. All together they hit 202 homers, a barrage that no doubt helped pitchers Dave Hillman and Gene Fodge pile up 40 victories between them.

"I might be prejudiced," Mauch says, "but I think it was the best minor league team ever put together. I saw some teams in the big leagues that couldn't play as well. Hell, I managed two of them." (Those would be the '61 Phillies and the '69 expansion Montreal Expos.) But there are still historians who believe the '34 Angels, winners of 137 games, losers of just 50, were superior. On the East Coast someone could surely beat the drum for the great Yankee farm teams at Newark in the '30s and '40s. But that was before my time; the '56 Angels were *of* it. And they captured my imagination as no team ever has – Bob Speake and Jim Bolger flanking Windy Wade in the outfield, Casey Wise turning double plays with Mauch, Elvin Tappe behind the plate, George Freese at the hot corner, and over at first . . . Bilko . . . Bilko . . . Bilko. . . .

You can always find naysayers who dismiss him as just another bush league vagabond, small minds that refuse to acknowledge the 20 homers he hit for Los Angeles in the expanded American League, know-nothings who close their ears when Mauch rhapsodizes about the big guy's grace and speed and athleticism. But I trust the way I feel about him enough to want it on the record: offer me 10 Mark McGwires and I would still rather have one Steve Bilko.

§ Once there were two ballparks.

Gilmore Field was the one with the drive-in movie behind its right-field wall. Gilmore Drive-In, predictably enough. Its proprietors, not being in the business of providing bonus entertainment for baseball fans, put up a protective screen on nights the Stars played. The only time anybody carped about it was when the game stank, inspiring chants to take the screen down. But few of the complainers were as enterprising as Art Spander, the *San Francisco Examiner* sports columnist who grew up watching the Stars and the Angels. "One night I went way down in the right-field bleachers and found a place where I could watch *The African Queen*," Spander says. It was a quintessentially Hollywood moment.

But when the film capital needed a ballpark for a movie, Wrigley Field usually got the call. It's there in *Damn Yankees* and *It Happens Every Spring* for the most logical of reasons: it looked like a big league stadium. And with 20,500 seats, it was meant to. When William Wrigley Jr. built the park for a million dollars in 1925, he modeled it after the one that bore his name in Chicago, right down to the ivy on the outfield wall. Funny thing, though: L.A.'s Wrigley Field had lights decades before Chicago's did.

"At Wrigley you felt like you were really uptown," says Max West, the former Boston Braves outfielder who finished his career with the Angels. "It was a far sight better than a lot of National League parks – Ebbets Field, Sportsman's Park in St. Louis, places like that."

But even if Wrigley had been a rock pile, West would have loved its 345-foot power alleys and its jet stream to right field. Without those advantages, West might not have put together back-to-back 35-homer seasons when his knees were crumbling beneath him. Nor would Mauch have hit more homers in three years as an Angel than he did in the rest of his 16 professional seasons combined. Take the time he tried to slap the ball to the right side to advance a runner, popped up, and was rewarded for his failure with an aerodynamic miracle. "The ball just kept carrying," Mauch says, "until it wound up in the bleachers." No wonder they shot TV's *Home Run Derby* at Wrigley.

At Gilmore the long ball was a much tougher proposition. In the park's 19-year history, Kelleher and Zernial were the only Stars with 40-homer seasons, and just three players – Luke Easter and two singles-hitting surprises, Lou Stringer and Bill Gray – were able to clear its towering center-field wall, 400 feet away. But talk of those wide-open spaces hard by the Farmers Market shouldn't fool you; Gilmore was really as cozy and intimate as a ballpark could be. It was built entirely of wood – no concrete, no girders – and when CBS's TV City went up next door in the early '50s, the ballpark's anachronistic charm was magnified. Gilmore sat only 12,000 people, so when the Stars and the Angels battled – a verb not used casually here – the Hollywood management had to rope off portions of the outfield to squeeze in the overflow crowd. But if you think the players had people breathing down their necks there, you should have seen the grandstand. Just 34 feet from home plate, just 24 feet from first and third bases, it brought new meaning to the term *tight quarters*. Pitchers thought the plate looked closer, base runners had to be careful not to wind up in the box seats when they rounded third, and hitters fouled out about as often as John Wayne performed Shakespeare.

You'll never hear anyone who played at Gilmore bad-mouth it. But when former players cite the reasons for their affection, they are usually careful to forget one. It has to do with the cracks between the park's wood planks and with the era's notion that women should wear dresses even to ball games. Contemplate that for a moment and you should realize why the players always spent the seventh-inning stretch under the stands.

§ Somewhere in my skimpy collection of Stars memorabilia is an 8 x 10 of a knuckleballer with the beguiling nickname of Kewpie Dick Barrett. What makes the picture so memorable is not the dimpled doll face perched atop his 45-year-old body. It's the short pants Kewpie Dick is wearing.

He was with Hollywood for only half of 1950, but he arrived just in time to take the mound with his knobby knees showing. The idea of dressing the Stars in shorts originated with – wouldn't you know it? – a sportswriter. After seeing British soccer teams wear shorts, Braven Dyer of the *Los Angeles Times* put the bug in Hollywood manager Fred Haney's ear. Flannel was baseball's fabric of choice back then, and in the summer it could turn a uniform into an oven. So Haney took a chance and sent his sheepish players onto the diamond with the breeze blowing up their britches.

"The nicest thing any of the other teams said to us was, 'Hello, sweetheart,'" former second baseman Gene Handley recalls.

Nobody rode the Stars with more delight than Oakland catcher Eddie Malone. "I called 'em a bunch of Boy Scouts," he says. A year later, however, Malone found himself playing for Hollywood. "The first time I walked in the clubhouse," he says, "the guys were all lined up, and there was Haney at the end of the line. He was holding a pair of them short pants. When he give 'em to me, he said, 'Now you're a member of the Scout troop.'"

As it turned out, Malone was more than happy to trade a few skinned knees for the drop in temperature when he played in shorts. Gilmore Field's female patrons certainly didn't mind the change in fashion, at least if you judged by the way they whistled at outfielder Clint Conatser. And Bill Veeck thought enough of the idea to borrow it in the late '70s, when he was making his last stand with the Chicago White Sox. But the Stars stayed with shorts for just three seasons before relegating them to the back of the closet.

If you want an epitaph for the experiment, Handley is happy to provide one: "Just another Hollywood stunt."

§ Carlos Bernier would be leading off first base and Gene Mauch would be scooping up a handful of dirt to throw in his face if he dared try stealing second. You knew that Bernier would and that the hostilities would escalate from there, for these were the Stars and the Angels, two teams that couldn't play a weeklong series without spilling blood. Even their radio announcers, the Angels' Bob Kelley and the Stars' Mark Scott, hated each other. So it's no surprise to hear that Bill Sweeney, when he managed the Angels, once offered a cashmere suit to the first man to start a fight with the Stars. But when Mauch waited four games before he tangled with Bernier, Sweeney withdrew the offer.

Maybe Mauch minded losing out on the suit all those years ago, but he doesn't anymore; indeed, he sounds like he got everything he wanted. "There was a high throw," he says, "and when I came down, I landed on Bernier. Just kind of walked all over him." The memory elicits a chuckle. "God, we had some fun back then."

If you measure fun in bruises and bloody noses, the Stars and the Angels may have had more of it than anybody. "Best rivalry I've ever seen, even better than the Dodgers and Giants," says Ben Wade, who formed his opinion while sandwiching a three-year stay in Brooklyn between two tours as a Star. Even when everybody knew the Dodgers would soon be moving to Los Angeles and there really wasn't anything left to fight for, you could still find southpaw pitcher Tommy Lasorda – yes, *that* Tommy Lasorda – knocking down the Stars' Spook Jacobs and Jacobs bunting the next pitch up the first-base line so he could get a piece of Lasorda. The result was a donnybrook for old times' sake. "Spook wound up going around the whole infield, swinging at everything in a gray uniform," says former Hollywood publicist Irv Kaze. But the beauty of the craziness between the Angels and the Stars was that it wasn't confined to red-asses like Lasorda and Jacobs, Mauch and Bernier. It worked like a full moon on even the gentlest souls.

Take burly Frank Kelleher, nicknamed Mousey by his Hollywood teammates and, in Handley's estimation, "as good a fella as ever lived." He wasn't any more of a brawler than Joe Hatten, the Angel left-hander who lived by his curveball, not his dukes. But after Kelleher got six straight hits against L.A. in '53, everybody in Gilmore Field's overflow crowd knew Hatten would have to forget his manners. He did it by burying a fastball in Kelleher's back.

When home plate umpire Cece Carlucci hustled to retrieve the ball, Kelleher charged the mound and threw a haymaker. "I thought it was Marciano," Carlucci says. "He hit Hatten in the chest. Must've knocked him 15 feet." The punch was a call to arms for a ruckus that lasted 10 minutes. When it was over, Carlucci gave Kelleher the thumb – "I don't think he'd ever been kicked out of a game before," the old ump says – and let Hatten remain because, what the hell, where's it written that a man can't pitch tight?

The Stars responded by sending little Ted Beard in to run for Kelleher. On the first pitch, Beard – who said hello on the first day of spring training, goodbye at the end of the season, and made the biggest noise of his career when he hit four home runs in a game in San Diego – stole second. On the next pitch, he lit out for third, where the Angels had stationed Murray Franklin, who had been a hero in Hollywood after his home run had clinched the 1949 pennant. But Beard apparently wasn't the sentimental type. He went into Franklin with his spikes "belly-button high," as the Stars' Stevens puts it. What followed was the mother of all free-for-alls.

Franklin and Beard proceeded to pound knobs on each other. Their teammates stormed out of the dugouts to do the same, almost gleefully. Kelleher and Malone, who were in the Hollywood clubhouse getting their wounds from the first fight patched up, raced back to join the action. Carlucci remembers the Stars' Handley and the Angels' Gene Baker looking "like a couple boxers going at each other." Not that Carlucci could admire them for long. "I was down three times," he says. And his fellow umpire Joe Iacovetti had to duck a roundhouse thrown by Angel catcher Al Evans. "We couldn't stop it," Carlucci says, and it was only a matter of time, he feared, before the fans would come piling in.

William Parker, L.A.'s chief of police, must have feared the same thing as he watched on TV because he wound up calling every available unit in the area to get to Gilmore. "I seen 'em coming from left field, right field, everywhere – 55 police officers," Carlucci says. "They got law and order for me." But not before a good half hour of war had been waged and photographers had the pictures that would fill three pages of *Life* magazine. And the second game of the doubleheader still had to be played.

They got it in with cops lining the dugouts and only nine players allowed out of each clubhouse at a time. Then Malone dragged his weary bones home and discovered that his kids had watched the whole thing on television. "They weren't sure what they'd seen because our TV was only about three inches big," Malone says, "so my daughter Gail, she asked me if I was in a fight, and I told her, 'Oh, no, honey, I wouldn't do that.'"

The next morning Malone was sleeping when he felt a tiny hand shake him. It was Gail, and she was holding a newspaper that had a picture of him throwing his Sunday punch.

"Daddy," she said accusingly, "you always told us to tell the truth."

§ The Stars did their damnedest to give Gilmore Field a Hollywood farewell, on September 5, 1957. They trotted out right-hander Hugh Pepper, and for 8 and 2/3 innings he held San Francisco hitless. Then the Seals' Ed Sadowski lined a clean single to remind everybody that happy endings are for the movies and bittersweet goodbyes are for real life.

Even though the Dodgers would come to Los Angeles in '58 and anoint it big time forever, something was being lost. The Stars and the Angels were leaving, and they were all I knew of baseball. Before the first wrecker's ball hit Gilmore, I could already feel the emptiness. I was not alone.

"For four or five years after the Dodgers came, I had this dream that there was still a Coast League team at Gilmore," says Allan Malamud, a neighborhood kid who grew up to be a *Los Angeles Times* sports columnist. "Every time I woke up, it killed me to find out I couldn't go to a game there."

Gilmore was long gone before Malamud stopped dreaming, leveled so CBS could have more space for parking and storage but not replaced until the network built a studio there last year. I suppose there is a natural progression to that, but I still like the way the lights went out on Wrigley Field better. For a while Walter O'Malley contemplated having the Dodgers play there, an idea he eventually scotched because of inadequate parking (unless, of course, you believe the story that he was offended by the presence of a whorehouse across the street). In any event the Dodgers ended up in the Coliseum, and Wrigley Field was without a team until the American League expanded in 1961 to embrace a collection of rejects, crazies, and wayfaring strangers who called themselves the Angels. They were only passing through, but before they closed the door behind them, their part-time first baseman hit the last home run in Wrigley Field's history. His name was Steve Bilko.

By 1966 Wrigley, too, was a memory, replaced by a community center honoring a city councilman who lived to be 90 and spent the last years of his life getting fleeced by a gold-digging girlfriend less than half his age. Just one more bittersweet touch, you might call it; one more metaphor for a city built on the young devouring the old.

But my supply of cynicism runs low when I think about the Stars and the Angels. If you judge by baseball's merciless yardstick, they never measured up to the Dodgers, but it was the Bilkos and Kellehers and Mauchs who showed me how wonderful the game could be, and I would never forget them. They were with me every time I went to see the big leaguers play that first season in the Coliseum, just as they were that fall when my parents told me we were moving to Salt Lake City. It was the beginning of a troubled time for me – three junior high schools in three years to compound all the usual turbulence and insecurity of adolescence. But Salt Lake was where the Stars had moved. Though they were known as the Bees now, there was no disguising Carlos Bernier in left field. And somehow, as I moved through my strange new world, trying to figure out who I was and who my friends were, that made everything all right.

Sports Illustrated, June 21, 1993

2

Laughing on the Outside

Picture this: a boy racing to the barbershop, reveling in his new-found freedom from his mother's hand, his pace accelerated by the thought that a black man's world is beckoning. There are no appointments at Scotty's, just three chairs and a wait that always eats up the clock. But the boy doesn't mind as long as the men are talking, and they always seem to be doing that, these cops, long-shoremen, and layabouts. Hour after hour they carry on as if there were no place they would rather be than here, where the only other sources of entertainment are a girlie calendar from *Jet* magazine and a transistor radio with a coat hanger for an antenna.

The men meander from topic to topic – politics, race, sex – and almost everything the boy hears is an education, especially about the action between the sheets. The one subject he feels fit to comment on is baseball. When the men ask him who his favorite players are, he has their names ready: Mays, Aaron, Clemente, and, oh yeah, Richie Allen. Got to put Allen in there because this is Philadelphia, and it's 1964, and he's hitting the ball so hard for the Phillies that he seems more an aspiring deity than a rookie.

Scotty gazes solemnly at the boy from behind the number one chair. He's the oracle of the shop, always has something certifiably intelligent to say, and when the boy looks back at him, Scotty seems as old as the blues, though he's probably only in his forties. "You never heard of Josh Gibson?" the barber asks.

The boy is puzzled. Why, no, he never has. And that is when the deluge begins. At first it's just Scotty, but pretty soon all the men are chiming in with stories. About Gibson hitting more homers than anybody – black, white, or whatever. About the way Gibson and Satchel Paige tuned each other up for the greater glory of the Negro leagues. About Gibson dying of a broken heart because he never got a chance to take a swing in the Jim Crow major leagues. About Gibson still having the last laugh because he pounded a home run clean out of Yankee Stadium, and nobody, not even Babe Ruth himself, ever did that.

As far as the men are concerned, you don't put any other hitter in the same sentence with Josh Gibson, least of all some damn rookie. When the boy finally leaves the barbershop, still trying to wrap his mind around everything he has heard, his one overriding thought is, Man, if this guy's better than Richie Allen. . . .

The boy will check for himself, for that is his nature long before he becomes known as Gerald Early, professor of English and African American studies at Washington University in St. Louis and author of an award-winning collection of essays, *The Culture of Bruising*. He has a passion for books and a trust in the wisdom they hold. So he goes to the library and digs out every volume of baseball history he can find. In none of them is there so much as a word about Gibson. All the stories that the men at the barbershop offered up as gospel might as well be vapor.

§ We know just enough about Josh Gibson now to forget him. It's a perverse kind of progress, a strange step up from the days when the mention of his name drew blank looks. He has been a Hall of Fame catcher since 1972, so that's a start. And you can always remind people that he got the Ken Burns treatment on public television, or that he was a character in an HBO movie, or that he inspired Negro leagues memorabilia harking back to his old ball club, the Homestead Grays. Any of it will do to jog memories. *Josh Gibson, sure. Hit all those home runs, didn't he?* Then he's gone once more, gone as soon as he's remembered.

It happened again in '98 and '99 as Mark McGwire and Sammy Sosa woke the long-ball ghosts with their history-making thunder. Suddenly the Babe and Roger Maris were leading a parade out of the shadows of the past, counting cadence for Hank Greenberg, Jimmie Foxx, and Mickey Mantle. Baseball grew misty over the musty, as only it can, and a grand time was had by all – except anyone who cared about Gibson.

He drew so few mentions that if you didn't know better, you would have wondered if he ever really picked up a bat. His obscurity recalled that of Jackie Robinson, a mystery to far too many African American ballplayers three years ago, on the 50th anniversary of his shattering of baseball's color line. But Robinson made it to the mountaintop, and in doing so he helped set the stage for Martin Luther King Jr. and Muhammad Ali, *Brown v. Board of Education*, and the *Civil Rights Act of 1964*. For Gibson, there was none of that, only booze and dope and busted dreams.

Whatever pain he died with lives on in the Negro leaguers who played with him, against him, and maybe even for him if they were fortunate enough to walk where he never could. "I almost hate to talk about Josh," says Hall of Famer Monte Irvin, who jumped from the Negro leagues to the New York Giants in 1949. "It makes me sad, for one thing, on account of he didn't get to play in the major leagues. Then, when you tell people how great he was, they think you're exaggerating."

But that's what greatness is: an exaggeration. Of talent, of charisma, of the acts that live long after the athletes we deem legendary have shuffled off this mortal coil. So it is with Gibson, who opened Irvin's eyes in 1937 by hitting a grounder so hard that it knocked the shortstop who caught it backward. Then there was the night in McKeesport, Pennsylvania, when Gibson bashed a homer and the mayor stopped the game until the ball was found, because he'd never seen one hit that far. "I played with Willie Mays and Hank Aaron," Irvin says. "They were tremendous players, but they were no Josh Gibson."

This is no different from Roy Campanella telling one and all that he couldn't carry Gibson's mitt. Or Walter Johnson arguing that Gibson was better than Bill Dickey in the days when Dickey was the benchmark for catchers. Or Dizzy Dean, a true son of the South, wishing his St. Louis Cardinals would sign Gibson – and Satchel Paige – so they could wrap up the pennant by the Fourth of July and go fishing until World Series time. Irvin, with his proclamation, leaves himself no wiggle room. He doesn't just count Gibson among the game's greats; he ranks him first.

To help make his case, Irvin paints a picture of a ninth-grade dropout from Pittsburgh who grew up to become John Henry in baseball flannels: 210 pounds of muscle sculpted on a 6-foot-2 frame, with the speed of a sprinter and a throwing arm that cut down would-be base stealers with lightning bolts. There is no mention of the fact that Gibson was less than artistic behind the plate – "a boxer" for the way he jabbed at the ball, in the estimation of his otherwise admiring former teammate Ted "Double Duty" Radcliffe. Likewise, Irvin remains silent on Gibson's struggles with pop-ups. Dwelling on shortcomings doesn't burnish a legend, and Irvin knows it. Better to concentrate on Gibson at the plate. "You saw him hit," Irvin says, "and you took your hat off."

You might even use that hat to fan yourself, so overheated are the statistics Gibson left behind: a .354 batting average for his 17 years in the Negro leagues, .373 for two summers in Mexico, .353 for two winters in Cuba. "Lifetime .300 and a whole lot," croons Buck O'Neil, the old Kansas City Monarch with the gift for euphonious phrasing. "He come up there right-handed, kind of a wide stance, didn't take much of a stride. But great shoulders, great wrists. Hit that ball a long way all over."

Gibson's statistical pinnacle was the .517 average he parked in the middle of the Grays' 1943 lineup. It looks like a typo, but *The Baseball Encyclopedia* says .517 is really what the man hit. He did it using bats and balls that were inferior to the ones big leaguers used. More significant, he did it with people arguing that his average wouldn't be so fat if he had to hit against white pitchers. These same doubters, however, never would have dreamed of belittling the Babe's 60 homers or Ted Williams's .406 season or Joe DiMaggio's 56-game hitting streak because they faced nary a pitcher of color. So maybe Gibson delivered his most important message by batting

.412 against the big leaguers on autumn barnstorming tours that the black teams dominated. Says O'Neil: "He wanted to prove he wasn't inferior to anybody."

Gibson made his point with his batting average and made it again by hitting so many home runs that only the blind and the bigoted dared ignore him. If you embrace everything you hear, there were 962 home runs – including 75 in 1931, 69 in 1934, and, brace yourself, 84 in 1936. But not even the greatest Gibson advocate will try to convince you that box scores are available to document all the homers with which Gibson is credited. Nor are you expected to believe that every pitcher to whom he laid waste was prime beef. There were too many games against semipros and independent teams, too many games played for the sole purpose of making enough money to get to the next backwater town and the next rocky diamond. That was life on the fringe, where black baseball existed.

Yet when Negro league teams went head-to-head, the competition matched that in the big leagues – and Gibson, predictably, was up to the challenge. Witness his 11 homers in 23 games in 1936, his 7 in 12 games in '37 and his 17 in 29 games in '39. "If you factored in what he did in league games over the old 154-game schedule," says Negro leagues historian John Holway, "he would have broken Ruth's record at least three times."

It is doubtful that any of the old-timers at Scotty's barbershop knew that or would have put much stock in it if they had. Statistics were for kids and white people. The barbershop regulars wanted something more out of baseball, something they could feel the way they felt a Charlie Parker saxophone solo. "They were like African Americans everywhere," Gerald Early says. "They connected to baseball in a different way from white Americans. They built stories, they built myths, and those tended to become the sole reality."

Thus the tale of how Gibson, alone among men, hit a home run out of Yankee Stadium. It would have been in September 1930, just months after he joined the Grays at age 18. They were playing the Lincoln Giants when he caught hold of a pitch thrown by the estimable Connie Rector and sent it soaring into never-never land. "I heard it bounced off the subway train," whispers Orlando Cepeda, sounding more like the awed child whose father played with Gibson in Puerto Rico than the slugger whose own plaque hangs in Cooperstown. Everybody has *heard* something about the homer – that's the problem. Nobody has ever found a shred of documentation, not even in a newspaper story about the game. The best guess is that the ball landed in the far reaches of the left center field bullpen. Not that saying so will stop anyone from telling the story. Not that anyone will cease using it as a springboard to all the other home runs that fueled Gibson's mythology.

Some homers you can document, like the one he launched out of Forbes Field in Pittsburgh, a feat duplicated by only a select group that includes Ruth and Willie Stargell. Other shots are forever confined to folklore, like the one that supposedly knocked a public address speaker off the grandstand roof in Washington's Griffith Stadium. "I didn't see it," confesses Don Newcombe, a workhorse right-hander for the Newark Eagles and the Brooklyn Dodgers, "but that's what the other players said." Of course they did.

Ninety-seven-year-old Double Duty Radcliffe – nicknamed by Damon Runyon after he pitched one game of a doubleheader and caught the other – is still telling people about an old lady who thought she was safe watching Gibson from the rocking chair on her front porch. "Wasn't no fence in this particular park," Radcliffe recalls. "Someplace in Pennsylvania, I think it was. She's out there in center field, rockin' away when Josh hits one. And . . . and. . . ." Radcliffe erupts in laughter made raspy by a lifetime of cigars. "Josh made that old lady jump."

But of all the stories inspired by Gibson's homers, one resonates most memorably about his life and times. It comes from an article his son, Josh Jr., clipped out of the *Pittsburgh Press* years ago. In it the retiring mayor of suburban Dormont talked of the day in 1933 that he saw Josh hit a home run out of the local ballpark, over a flagpole, and across a street, 470 feet if it was an inch. There were 500 people in the stands, but when they passed the hat, $66 was the best they could come up with in the heart of the Depression. The umpires and ball chasers got paid first, and the two teams had to divvy up the $44 that remained. Josh's share was $1.67.

§ It was a life on the run, and in the days when he could get away with ignoring real-life complications, he thrived on it. Didn't matter how many whistle-stops he rolled into in the dead of night, or how many bug-infested hotels he slept in, or how many times he was turned away from restaurants by the same white people who cheered his slugging. Josh was going to be Josh: a muscle-stuffed scamp who teased opposing batters by throwing dirt on their shoes and who menaced pitchers by rolling up his sleeves to show off his biceps.

He never said much, but talking wasn't his game. Hitting was. When he had finished another day's work at the plate, he would climb back onto the bus that was his cocoon. It seemed as if nothing could touch him there. All he had to do to keep his teammates happy was lean out the window when they passed another ball club's bus and say what he always said: "Same team won today is gonna win tomorrow." Hell, it even kept the other ball club happy. This wasn't just anybody needling them. It was Josh Gibson.

They called him "the black Babe Ruth," but he was more than that. He was a 1,000-watt celebrity in the parallel universe that spawned him, and his star shone brightest whenever he rolled into one of the big cities on the Negro leagues' endless caravan: New York or D.C. or sweet home Pittsburgh. He would hit the jazz clubs then, places that were to black players what Toots Shor's was to the Yankees, and he would rub shoulders with Lena Horne, Duke Ellington, and the Mills Brothers as if they were old friends. After a while maybe they were, because they let Gibson get up and sing with the band, sing something smoky or swinging in that rich voice of his.

Pittsburgh's hot club was the Crawford Grille, up on what the locals still know as "the Hill." Gus Greenlee ran it with money he made in the numbers racket, and when he branched out into the Negro National League, he bought Gibson. And Paige. And fearsome, hard-hitting Oscar Charleston. They were the engine that drove the Pittsburgh Crawfords in the '30s, and surely they would have lasted far longer if Greenlee hadn't run afoul of the IRS. Then, in 1937, Gibson went back to the Homestead Grays, back where he had started and where he would finish.

There was heartbreak at both ends of his journey, though the focus usually falls on his premature death at 35. Overlooked too often is what he had faced 17 years earlier, when he was just a kid with a big future in baseball and a pregnant girlfriend who became his wife. The former Helen Mason was 17 when she gave birth to twins, then died before she could hold them in her arms.

From that day forward Gibson didn't stop running until he, too, was in his grave. Fatherhood scarcely slowed him. Indeed, it might have done just the opposite. Says James A. Riley, director of research for the Negro Leagues Baseball Museum in Kansas City: "Every time he saw those kids, he thought of his wife." The thought, if you accept Riley's theory, was more than Gibson could bear.

His wife's family fought to change his rambling ways. They were strong Baptists who had been lured out of the South by the clang of Pittsburgh's steel mills, just the way Gibson's family had. The Masons weren't about to stand by while Gibson chose a mere game over the son who bore his name and the daughter who bore Helen's. "There was incredible bitterness," says Ken Solarz, the Hollywood screenwriter who sent a love letter to the Negro leagues with his 1979 documentary *Only the Ball Was White*. "Can you imagine what it was like when his wife's family told him he had to quit baseball and raise those children? It must have been devastating."

It was also ineffective. Josh Jr., 69 and twice the recipient of a kidney transplant, approaches the issue gingerly, conceding only that he was raised by his maternal grandmother and that growing up, he didn't see much of his father. "They used to say the Negro leagues never dropped the ball," Josh Jr. says, "so my father, he was always off playing somewhere." Big Josh spent his summers stateside, coming back to Pittsburgh every two weeks or so. In the winters he set sail for Latin America and the paydays to be had there. When he returned, it was always with gifts. "Good leather stuff for me and my sister," Josh Jr. says. An empty, groping moment passes. "And we were glad to see him."

The awkwardness of those words is amplified when the son recalls how he and his sister romped in a field across the street from the house where their father lived with his common-law wife. "We never knew her name," Josh Jr. says.

He thought things would change when he turned 11 and big Josh invited him to travel with the Grays as their batboy for two weeks. This was to be the bonding mechanism for father and son, a ritual that would continue for the next three summers. When Josh Jr. thinks back, however, his memories run mainly to his father's home runs, the art of living on $2 a day in meal money, and riding the team bus with the legend who begat him. They were supposed to sit together up front, Josh and Junior, but once the bus was on the road, the boy always found himself alone. His father had left him to play gin rummy in the back with the other Grays. It didn't matter where big Josh was; he couldn't stop running.

§ It's a different kind of crack of the bat. I'll tell you what, you listen to a .22 rifle, and then you listen to a .30-30. That's the difference right there.
– Buck O'Neil

If you insist on calling the story that follows apocryphal, keep in mind that Buck O'Neil has been dining out on it for years, and he isn't about to stop. It begins sometime in the 1920s with Buck lurking behind the outfield fence in Sarasota, Florida, fresh out of the celery fields where he usually toiled and surrounded by kids as hungry as he was. They were there to track down the balls that sailed over the fence and sell them to tourists eager for spring training souvenirs. Never mind that the Yankees had rolled into town with their Murderers' Row. This was strictly business.

And then it wasn't. As the longest ball of the day soared into view and the take-no-prisoners race for it began, Buck stood stock still, mesmerized by the crack of the bat. "Oh, a beautiful sound," he says more than 70 years later, as rhapsodic as if he'd been the first to hear Heifetz or Hendrix. In an instant Buck was climbing the nearest pine tree, going up the wooden slats the kids had nailed into it as steps so they could watch games without paying. "When I got to the top," he says, "I saw this guy with a big barrel chest and skinny legs and a beautiful swing." Dramatic pause. "It was Babe Ruth."

A decade or so later, O'Neil was the Kansas City Monarchs' first baseman, and the first time he suited up in Griffith Stadium to face the Grays, he heard it again: that wondrous sound. "So I ran out of the clubhouse, through the dugout, and onto the field," O'Neil says. "There was this beautiful black sucker. Big chest, broad shoulders, about 34 inches in the waist. That was Josh Gibson. Hitting the ball, making it sound just like Babe Ruth. I'm standing there taking it all in when I hear people laughing, people applauding. I look around, trying to find out what's the matter, and one of my teammates says, 'Buck, you got nothing on but your jockey strap.'"

O'Neil returned to the clubhouse embarrassed but wiser, for he knew he had the perfect standard for assessing sluggers. They had to match the Babe's sound – and Josh's. If you think it's easily done, be advised that when O'Neil traveled to St. Louis last year, Mark McGwire flunked the test.

§ Oh, there were some players back in the day – Cool Papa Bell and Mule Suttles, Ray Dandridge, Leon Day, and Martin Dihigo. Legions of them when you get right down to it: men who make you want to weep for having missed out on seeing the Negro leagues. Yet the two names you always come back to in any discussion of that star-crossed age are the same ones that were on the billboards that shouted, SEE SATCHEL PAIGE STRIKE OUT THE 1ST NINE HIT-TERS! SEE JOSH GIBSON HIT TWO HOMERS!

Satch and Josh were as big as the type that promised these heroics, for both of them had moved beyond mere greatness into walking immortality. "Emblematic," Gerald Early calls them. "They repre-sented the mythology of the Negro leagues." But when they played together on the Crawfords, everyone had five years to study how different they were as human beings.

"Josh rode the team bus; Satch drove his own car," James A. Riley says. "Josh showed up at the park when he was supposed to; Satch might not show up at all. Satch was a modern ballplayer before there were modern ballplayers." Gibson was a mystery, no matter how good natured and playful he was. He would win a game with a homer and have a beer with the guys afterward, but then, if there wasn't a bus to catch and another game waiting at the end of an all-night drive, he would be gone, off into a world of his own, a world he didn't share. Of course Satch never noticed, as caught up as he was in his own magnitude. There were years when he won 70 games (by his count), and his singleness of purpose suggested that he was sizing Gibson up as an opposing hitter even when they were teammates. That was the only mystery Satch cared about.

He told Gibson as much, bless his heart, and both of them would sit there laughing, woofing, each promising to inflict unspeakable cruelty on the other. When these icons finally went head-to-head, in 1942, the showdown entered the mythos. It was mostly Satch's doing. That cunning rogue was pitching for Kansas City, and, according to legend, when he was one out from beating the Grays, he ignored the runner on third and walked the next two hitters for the express purpose of facing his old teammate. Gibson was so stunned that he watched three straight strikes, the last one on a fastball Satch called "a bee at your knee."

Satch acted as if that gave him bragging rights till the end of time. Josh never said much about it, but he did sidle up to Monte Irvin not long afterward and confide, "Satch is crazy." Publicly, that was all Gibson's pride would allow. Privately, it may have needed balm. Why else would one of the few newspaper clippings he saved be about the day he went 4-for-4 against Satch at Wrigley Field? Gibson did the same against lots of pitchers, but this was special; this was the great Paige. While he was on base that day, Gibson might even have taunted his fellow legend by hooting, "If you could cook, I'd marry you." If he didn't say it that time, he said it later, or so the story goes. He always did enjoy beating Satch like a rented mule.

§ It was strange having Josh around that winter. In the past he had headed south on the first thing smoking as soon as the Negro leagues' season was done, not to return until winter was melting. But after he had taken his last swing for the Grays in 1946 and gone to Latin America, illness made him retreat to the row house on Pittsburgh's Bedford Avenue, where his mother-in-law was raising his kids. Once he was there, nothing could get him to leave.

Sam Bankhead, his teammate, drinking buddy, and best friend, thought it was just a matter of time before Gibson caved in to the old lures of Caribbean rum, dark-eyed women, and December sunshine. "You ain't going back, Josh?" Bankhead kept asking, teasingly at first, then with more and more dismay as he realized that no, Josh wasn't going back. He was getting ready to die.

He had puffed up to 235 pounds, his knees were shot, and the rest of his once proud body was sending distress signals. He had high blood pressure and a brain tumor that periodically leveled him with headaches. He drank too much, and there was talk that he had found another escape route in drugs. He had woman problems and psychiatric problems. It was no kind of shape for a legend to be in as he turned 35.

How odd – and unfortunate – that even today there are those who want to blame Gibson's demise on the ascension of Jackie Robinson. It's so easy, so poetic to say that Gibson died of a broken heart when he realized that baseball's color line would be broken without him in the spring of '47. "That," Early insists, "has been romanticized way out of proportion."

Josh Jr. agrees, and so do most of the Negro leaguers who remember his father best. Talk to them for five minutes, and without prompting, they'll bring up their chagrin at the 1996 HBO movie *Soul of the Game*, which portrays Josh, Satch, and Jackie as friends and rivals. "My father didn't even know Jackie Robinson," says Josh

Jr. The inaccuracy is compounded when the movie shows the elder Gibson belittling Robinson as a "house nigger."

"I asked the producers where they got their information," O'Neil says, "and they said, Ernie Banks's son. I said, 'Ernie Banks's son? He wasn't even born yet.'"

If Gibson was crushed by anything beyond his own demons, it wasn't bitterness but disappointment. For too many years his hopes had been raised by the praise of big league managers who coveted his talent, then dashed by the cowardice of team owners afraid to be the first to challenge the game's racist status quo. When Leo Durocher, the Dodgers' manager, dared muse in the early '40s about the joy of writing Gibson's name on his lineup card, commissioner Kenesaw Mountain Landis dressed him down. The Pittsburgh Pirates and the Washington Senators also backed off when confronted by the bushy-browed Landis, who preached that there was white baseball and there was black baseball, and never would they meet. The teams got the message, and so did Gibson. "Finally," Riley says, "I think he just said, 'The hell with it.'"

Gibson's beverage of choice changed from beer to hard liquor. "Sometimes you could smell him from the night before," Don Newcombe remembers. "It was coming out his pores."

Radcliffe carries the same memory of Gibson. "He was smokin' that reefer too," Duty says.

Many old-timers trace Gibson's problems to a D.C. mobster's wife named Grace. Her husband was in the army, and Gibson had drifted apart from the woman who shared his bed in Pittsburgh. Things just went from there, drugs and passion fueling Josh and Grace's relationship until the mobster came home and reclaimed his lady. Then Josh was back on his own, and it must have been a scary place to be. There were stays at St. Elizabeth's, a mental hospital in Washington that let him out only for games on weekends. And there were myriad stories about his bizarre behavior, beginning with the one about the teammate who found him talking to a Joe DiMaggio who wasn't there.

Cepeda swears Gibson got arrested in Puerto Rico for running the streets naked. Newcombe remembers how bad he and the other Newark Eagles felt for laughing at a story imported from Latin America about how Gibson slid in with a double and started looking for the potatoes he said he had planted under second base. "We wanted to be proud of Josh Gibson," Newcombe says.

By the mid-'40s, however, Gibson may not have even been proud of himself. The knees that had kept him out of World War II were so bad that it hurt to watch him trying to crouch behind home plate. Though he had won home run championships in 1944 and '45 and batted .361 in '46, the power and menace of old were gone. So he took refuge in the home where his children lived, and he even slept in the same bed with Josh Jr. "I'd get up in the morning and go to school," his son recalls. "He'd get up and go wherever he wanted to."

On January 20, 1947, almost a month to the day after his 35th birthday and three months before Jackie Robinson made his historic debut with the Dodgers, Josh went to his mother's house, and it was there that he died. Some say a stroke killed him, others a brain hemorrhage. Or maybe it was just life.

Death didn't treat him any better, letting him lie in an unmarked grave in Allegheny Cemetery for nearly three decades. Finally, commissioner Bowie Kuhn joined with one of Gibson's Crawfords teammates in 1975 to buy the headstone his family couldn't afford. It hails him as a LEGENDARY BASEBALL PLAYER, but the words seem too spare, too perfunctory. How much closer to the truth Newcombe comes when he says, "It's too bad Josh didn't get a chance to live the life he should have lived."

§ They don't talk about Josh Gibson much in barbershops anymore. Too many years have passed; too many other great players have come down the pike; too many other shooting stars have flamed out. Even in Pittsburgh, the launching pad for his greatness, he remains little more than an afterthought. Mario Lemieux has a street named after him, and Roberto Clemente is honored by a park and a bridge. For years, all Gibson had was a blue-and-gold plaque designating the site where he played at Greenlee Field, up on the

Hill. The plaque isn't much bigger than a NO PARKING sign, and the Historical Society of Western Pennsylvania didn't get around to putting it up until 1996.

This year Gibson's likeness appeared on a downtown mural, but even so, all he really has going for him is his son. "I got to keep my father's name ringing," Josh Jr. says. From his Pittsburgh home he travels anywhere he is invited: minor league ball games, Negro leagues reunions, the Florida Marlins' opening day ceremonies last year and, most of all, baseball card shows. Alas, he doesn't have much to offer in the way of memorabilia – no bats that big Josh used, no catcher's mitts, no spikes with their toes curling. "The only thing I have of my father's are old newspaper articles he saved," Josh Jr. says. So he puts the articles in a display case, signs autographs for $25 a shot, and tells stories about the father who died when he was 16 and left him with a name that has proved as much a burden as a blessing.

"It wasn't easy trying to be Josh Gibson," his son says. Josh Jr. inherited his father's resonant voice and not much else in the way of natural gifts. He lacked size, power, and a flair for the dramatic. The best thing he could do as a spindly third baseman was run, and that ended after he left the Homestead Grays in 1959 for Canada's Provincial League. He broke an ankle stealing a base and tried to keep playing by deadening the pain with novocaine. When he could run no more, he limped home to a city job slinging trashcans. The job lasted until one of his kidneys gave out 20 years ago, and his struggle intensified in 1983, when hypertension cut short his twin sister's life.

But keeping his father's name alive has given Josh Jr. a reason to soldier on. He travels with his grandson Sean, who, at 30, looks like big Josh: same heft, same round face, same easy smile. "He's learning history," Josh Jr. says, "because he's going to take over when I die."

The two started a Josh Gibson League for kids in Pittsburgh last year, giving those youthful dreamers a place to learn about the Negro leagues and rack up their own hits, runs, and errors. A place where they can hear Josh Jr. say, "The thing I don't like particularly is that people call my father the black Babe Ruth. I'd prefer it if they just called him Josh Gibson."

It is an understandable request, but the truth is, Gibson must be remembered before he can be called anything. In that regard, there is only so much reassurance Josh Jr. can offer himself. He can tell the story of how Johnny Bench stopped him at a card show and said he wished he'd seen big Josh play: one great catcher paying homage to another. Or he can pass along the tales told by the men who played with his father. Mainly it comes down to Josh Jr. sitting at the table in his cramped dining room, pulling something from an envelope, and saying, "Here, I got to autograph this for you."

It is a picture of big Josh with the Grays in his prime, his arms thick, his smile shy, almost beguiling. Very carefully, Josh Jr. writes his name in blue ink across his father's shoulder. When a legend is on life support, you do what you have to.

Sports Illustrated, June 26, 2000

3

Hit and Run

Wings and Prayers

As easy as it is to do, giving your dreams over to baseball can be a hard thing, too. The men I offer as proof in these four short pieces weren't all found on wind-cursed diamonds or in cold-water clubhouses. They crossed my path in offices, at parties, even at a documentary screening. Which is to say that baseball's dreamers are everywhere among us and that the dream never really dies.

The Right-hander

The right-hander has had his ticket for weeks, and New Year's morning he will be gone. There will be no more throwing inside a gym three days a week, no more lifting weights on three others, no more lonely jogs through Chicago's slushy streets. American Airlines flight 107 is going to carry him to Phoenix and the kind of dream I'm glad kids still have.

Although he is 22 years old, the owner of a college degree, and a certified shareholder in America's future, the right-hander wants nothing more right now than the chance to play pro ball. He wants it so badly that he is willing to take this great leap across the country and fork over $500 for the privilege of spending two weeks at the Wally Moon Baseball School. "At first I planned on going for one week," the right-hander says, "but Wally Moon wrote and said it would be better if I was there for the whole shot." And the right-hander, in the sweet innocence born of great expectations, still can't see anything cynical in the suggestion.

Maybe it is better that way. Maybe the focus John Ruane has on his dream as a right-hander won't get distorted if he refuses to think of Moon as anything but a potential benefactor. Surely it is more pleasant for Ruane to listen to his elders talk about old Wally as a heavy hitter renowned for two things – hitting home runs over the Los Angeles Coliseum's infamous left-field screen and having a solitary eyebrow that ran all the way across his forehead.

The stories make me realize how old I am getting and how young Ruane is. To him, Wally Moon isn't one of yesterday's heroes; he is somebody with today's connections. "He owns the Double A club in San Antonio," Ruane tells me, "and he has all the contracts on the Salem, Oregon, club. I figure he ought to be able to send me somewhere." After all, he has done it before. He even did it for a guy Ruane played ball with last summer.

That's where Ruane gleaned the idea for his great adventure. He was working out of the bullpen for a semipro team called the Stallions on the Southwest Side, and he kept hearing a pitcher named Mark Adams talk about going to the Wally Moon school and playing with Salem. "He stayed there about four weeks," Ruane says, "and then he had arm problems and they had to let him go." But so what? Adams had drawn the paycheck that made him a bona fide professional; he had been between the white lines of what the *Sporting News* so reverently calls "Organized Baseball"; he had sampled the rarefied atmosphere that Ruane yearns to know first-hand and that I only heard about from teammates and opponents with gifts I never had.

Two of them – George Theodore and Doug Howard – levitated all the way to the big leagues. The others left in glory and drifted back in various states of repair. Even the worst cases had it over me, however, for I was planted behind home plate, a catcher with a good arm and bad eyes, leaden legs, and a bat with holes in it. "How was it?" I'd ask. The answers I got sounded like poetry.

There was the pitcher who realized that his future lay in dentistry after Jim Wynn drilled his best fastball through the sodden air of a Florida summer. And what about the two hellions the Mets shipped to Salinas, California, only to discover that no outfield would be big enough to hold them both? They were the complete opposite of the devout Mormon third baseman who quit the Tigers' organization because he thought the devil had a hold on too many of his teammates. And nobody could ever be quite like the first baseman who astounded his fellow Cardinal farmhands by emptying half a bottle of ketchup over his green beans before gobbling them down.

The characters in my private drama may never have realized it, but they were part of something that struck me as quintessentially American. I thought it took a pioneer's spirit and instinctive sense of romance to toss your glove and spikes into an old suitcase and go off to play baseball in small towns where you eat cheeseburgers at every meal and curse the boarded-up movie house. Indeed, I still do. But when the minor leagues began to shrink, my faith wavered. I imagined potential baseball wanderers rejecting their calling and becoming accountants or lawyers or, God forbid, sportswriters.

Now John Ruane tells me that I need not fret. He knows one kid who signed with the Expos and another who signed with the Blue Jays, and he himself is willing to sign with any team that will have him.

"I throw harder than most people around here," he says. "I got clocked at 85 miles an hour at one of those tryout camps where 3,000 guys show up. They're a waste of time, you know that? The tryout camps, I mean. The Major League Scouting Bureau had one at McKinley Park once, and I got pulled aside so they could take my picture with all the scouts. They took my name and address, too, so I kinda thought something was going to happen. Nah, I never heard from anybody."

The silence could have destroyed Ruane's dream. Instead, it only made the dream bigger. If Ruane has any down moments, they revolve primarily around the time he frittered away playing hockey and the porous infield that made him look so vulnerable when he pitched his senior year at Chicago State. The rest of the time, however, he has been busy listening to his girlfriend tell him he can play pro ball, bending the ear of every baseball man he can locate, and driving toward the end of a rainbow. It was supposed to be in Bakersfield, California, where an independent minor league team awaited whatever talent turned up on its doorstep. But by the time Ruane got there, the team was gone.

So he took his English degree and got a job in the Sun-Times sports department answering the phones, punching box scores into the computer, and, mainly, waiting until he could start the New Year right. He will get off at 11 Wednesday night, and nine hours later, he will be on the plane to Phoenix. He's not even sure if there will be anybody to meet him at the airport, but that really doesn't matter.

One way or another, when the Wally Moon Baseball School opens for business Friday, John Ruane will be there. I wish I was going with him.

Chicago Sun-Times, December 31, 1980

AUTHOR'S NOTE: John Ruane never got that pro contract. Just when Wally Moon was ready to sign him to one, he ruined his right shoulder in a collision at home plate and saw his dream die. Now he runs a thriving public relations agency in Atlanta, coaches kids' teams, and says his teenaged son throws harder than he ever did.

Out in the Cold

He used to laugh at snowy days in February. He used to dare them to hit him with their best shot because he wasn't going to be around for target practice much longer. Pitchers and catchers had to report to Florida early, and if there was one order he loved to obey, that was it. Even when the sun had roasted his neck and he didn't think he could run another wind sprint, life between baseball's white lines beat shoveling snow. He thinks about that a lot now that he doesn't have spring training to rescue him from the cold, now that he is 28 and a pitcher no more.

The end came last season. There was too much pain in his right shoulder and not enough heat in his fastball, so the big club wrote the obituary for his career and stuck it in the filing cabinet where it will sit forevermore. Just like that, he was finished. He had never made the majors, had never even pitched an inning up there, and in less time than he ever needed to warm up, he learned that he never would.

It took him an eternity to accept destiny's decree. Maybe he should have been better prepared; after all, his shoulder had been torturing him since the day he signed a professional contract, and on those rare occasions when the pain eased up, it got rerouted to his elbow. But the heart doesn't always heed what the head tells it. That's the curse of being young, gifted, and open to compliments. From the beginning, he listened to the praise of his teammates and the hitters he overpowered, he saw the bleachers overflow with big league scouts in search of a special magic, and he took their message literally: he couldn't miss.

The words still echoed through his head when he was hanging around the house with no contract, no job outside baseball, and no real interest in using his college degree to get one. Even now that he has been lured into the nine-to-five world, he seems almost embarrassed about it. "I didn't really want to go to work," he says, "but. . . ." His shrug speaks volumes. It is time to forge into the future, time to forget what he might have been. He crosses his fingers and waits. And suffers.

You wonder if he would find any consolation in knowing that Mickey Mantle is suffering, too. It's all in the latest *Esquire* – the old Yankee slugger wishing he could be young again, trying to make his way in a world he can't really deal with, drinking too much and remembering how it felt to be the toast of New York. But there is a difference between having what you wanted and losing it, and simply never having had it. At least Mickey Mantle knows what the top is like. To the pitcher whose dreams died young, it will always be a mystery and a torment.

He played out his career on bumpy minor league diamonds, under flickering lights, in front of empty stands. Even when he pitched a no-hitter in Triple A, it seemed like a secret. Sure, the local paper fussed over him the next day and he got a mention in the *Sporting News*, but in the world at large, only devotees of trivia knew he was out there swimming upstream.

If he enjoyed what could be called a crowning achievement, it was that he kept his head above water for six years. In an age when prospects and suspects alike are in training camp one week, on a bus to Dubuque the next week, and back home the week after that, he endured because the big club's brass had dreams as grand as his. They had seen his fastball take off and fly when the pain in his shoulder declared one of its rare cease-fires. They had seen him pitch as well as any of the kids who helped make the big club a champion last year. They had seen everything but the possibility that he would wind up in a corner at a party, nursing a beer and trying to laugh away the blues that baseball gave him.

He showed up with his wife and a handful of the guys he had

played with in high school, friends who have always been there, confidantes who don't demand a constant song-and-dance from him. Maybe he wouldn't even have talked about his broken dream if the conversation hadn't swung to athletes and the curious lives they lead. Once he started, though, nobody in the corner wanted to hear about anything else.

It didn't matter that he claimed to have pitched the worst complete game in the history of organized baseball – a 10–6 victory in Ashville, North Carolina – or that Mike Schmidt once hit his best fastball off his fists and still turned it into a home run. He was special because he had a talent that thousands of kids only pray for, and even now he doesn't start seeming human until he gets around to discussing the pain that reduced him to mere mortality.

There wasn't a trainer anywhere who was able to prescribe anything for it except rubbing alcohol. Even the doctors he went to couldn't help him. They tried surgery, and when that failed, they accused him of hypochondria, and when that sent him into a rage, they told him to rest. So he did, for six months, and when he came back and threw, the pain was still there, a devil stabbing him with a pitchfork.

Now that he doesn't make his living on a baseball diamond anymore, the pain has shifted to another part of his body. When there are games on television, he can deal with the picture but not the sound. He has to listen to music, has to keep moving – anything to keep him from getting wrapped up in the action. It seems eerie, but it is nothing his friends didn't expect. They remember the year his aching shoulder forced him out of uniform in mid-season. He came home to lick his wounds, and only to keep peace in the old neighborhood did he agree to go down to Comiskey Park to watch the White Sox play the team he would never make.

"It drove me crazy," he said as the memory invaded his corner of the party. "Absolutely crazy."

"Why?" asked a woman who had been listening to him.

"Because I should have been out there."

Chicago-Sun Times, February 11, 1981

Fathers and Sons

Fathers tend to make too much of baseball, as if the game were some sort of holy grail and the men who play it were guaranteed an immortality beyond that which the record book provides. To the dreamers who beget us, everything can be Reggie Jackson hitting home runs that never come down or Fernando Valenzuela bending his curveball around every bat in sight. Overlooked are the bush league bus rides, the arms that ache like rotting teeth, and the secrets these fathers' sons tell each other once they have arrived in the land of carpeted clubhouses.

They speak softly, but in the quiet that exists three hours before a game, when the rest of the team is just leaving the hotel and the volume on the TV hasn't been turned up yet, their words carry like baseballs in thin air. Even if you didn't include eavesdropping as one of your professional skills, you couldn't help but hear the outfielder when he asked, "Your boy playing ball?"

The catcher's words became distinct as soon as he stopped polishing his black loafers to answer: "Nah, he's got another year before he's old enough. How about yours?"

"If he wants to. That's what I tell him."

The catcher raised his eyes in mild surprise. "Your dad push you about playing?"

"Yeah. Yours too?"

"My dad said I wasn't gonna amount to anything if I didn't play all the damn time."

"Same thing I heard. I could play all day, and when my dad came home from work, he didn't want to hear about it. He'd drag me out for another couple hours. Wore my ass out."

"He a ballplayer?"

"Yeah. Another catcher. But he never went anywhere. Just wanted me to be what he wasn't, I guess."

"I know what you mean. Scares me to even think about it."

"So what do you tell your kid?"

"I tell him, 'Chris, you want to play ball, then play ball. You want to go fishing, then go fishing.' Simple as that."

The catcher nodded as if it really were and started shining his shoes again.

Maybe he will be able to get away with using the outfielder's prescription for sanity, but he has the edge on most fathers his age. He has been to the top of baseball's mountain, and he knows the trip isn't necessarily worth the price everyone who takes it may have to pay. There are too many hurts and heartaches that go unheeded by the people in the stands, too many slings and arrows to rain down upon kids who don't want to test their armor against them.

In the love that fathers have to give their sons, the love we think of most on Father's Day, good men can go blind. They can get the idea that they are somehow falling short of what is expected if they merely buy their boys grandstand seats, nudge them when Carl Yastrzemski comes to bat, or hurry home with them so they can play catch just for fun. Fun is what baseball is for, of course – for remembering the crew cut Pete Rose wore as a rookie or reciting the lead Red Smith wrote after watching the home run that assured Bobby Thomson of everlasting fame. But good men can forget it all once they start picturing their sons in the heroes' roles.

It happens in every sport. The aims start high and the values end up low. There are boxers whose fathers steal money from them, basketball players whose fathers want to go whoring with them, and football players whose fathers put a price tag on them. But baseball is the sport where sensibilities seem to get stood on end most often. Not the worst sport, mind you – not the worst by any means. Just the one that fathers know best and fall for hardest.

You remember the way it was when your own father was sitting high in the grandstand at your American Legion games and watching the madness 10 rows below him. He was an immigrant and just happy to have seen Gabby Hartnett's Homer in the Gloamin'. Though he hoped you were good at the sport he had come to love, he didn't have the gall to plead your case out loud. Would that your team's other fathers could have shared his gentle silence.

But one filled himself with vodka and the air with propaganda. Another flashed his wallet and put the team in new uniforms and his blushing son at first base. And the worst of all never paused to remember that he already had driven the best athlete in his family to a rubber room. He spit on his hands, hitched his pants, and uttered a shameless prayer that the next son off his assembly line wouldn't be such a butterfly. Never did he feel the hurt eyes of his kin or sense the bewilderment with which outsiders greeted him season after season. He had to create a major leaguer in his image. Thank God he never succeeded.

Perhaps he understands now that such things are rarely planned. If he doesn't, he should talk to the third baseman who gets nervous when friends tell him how smoothly his eight-year-old son fields ground balls and how it won't be long before some team is waving a contract under the kid's nose. It is a pleasant mixture of praise and good humor, but the third baseman can feel his vocal cords constricting. "I . . . I . . . I don't even want to talk about that," he says. Because the life he is considering isn't his own; it is his son's. And all he can give it, as a father, is all any father should give – love.

Chicago Sun-Times, June 20, 1982

Baseball without Justice

In a world where justice doesn't always embrace the right people, Jimmie Crutchfield closes his eyes and smiles a lot. It is enough for him to remember that he was in the same lineup with the great Josh Gibson and that on the last galloping catch he ever made, in 1945, a startled rookie gushed that Joe DiMaggio himself couldn't have done any better.

And yet Crutchfield, on those rare occasions when he has an audience, doesn't dally over such praise as lovingly as you might expect. "I'm kinda shy about things like that," he says. He would do well to add *proud* to his description of his feelings, for this is a man who typifies the strength and dignity of the Negro leagues, the baseball showcases that white America ignored until they were dead and gone.

Crutchfield would not bend under the weight of prejudice, nor would he beg or whimper. For 16 seasons, with the Birmingham Black Barons, the Pittsburgh Crawfords, and the Chicago American Giants, he found a sense of purpose in a society seemingly determined to strip him of his manhood. "We had ball games to worry about," he says. "We didn't have time to hate people."

Now, at a time when confrontation is fashionable, his attitude comes across as timid, even Uncle Tomish. But Crutchfield refuses to be cowed. He is nobody's pantywaist, and if you doubt that, consider his long-term silence on the golden years of his youth. It was as if he wasn't going to share his memories with the world because the world had once been so disinterested. So he sealed his lips for a decade. How hard that must have been for someone fairly bubbling with charm and good humor. But the other clerks at Chicago's main post office might never have discovered his past if a magazine story hadn't blown his cover.

"Hey, Crutch," a friend said. "I didn't know you played ball."

"Yeah," he replied. "A little."

It was the beginning of the steady stream of attention that has followed Jimmie Crutchfield into this, his 70th, year on the planet. And truth be known, he has enjoyed it at times. There was, for example, a sportswriter at a small New Jersey newspaper who had 400 postcard-size pictures of him printed up so he would have something to autograph. "I get lots of letters from kids who read about me," Crutchfield says, "and this way I can send them something I can't really afford myself."

Just the same, doubt never let him out of its clutches. He would always wonder what the writers who talked to him were doing with the only treasure he had. From other old Negro leaguers, he would hear horror stories about the priceless photographs that were borrowed and never returned. His reaction, naturally enough, was to clam up again.

Only the most resolute and sincere truth-seekers could get to him after that, and Ken Solarz, a producer from Channel 11, Chicago's PBS station, is nothing if not resolute and sincere. He knocked on Crutchfield's door on the South Side and wouldn't go away until he had what he wanted. The proof that the wait was worth it shines through *Only the Ball Was White*, Solarz's bittersweet 30-minute documentary about the grit and beauty that was black baseball.

That is not to say, however, that Crutchfield is the only star in the show. He shares the spotlight with the wide-eyed, innocent Roy Campanella and the eccentrically wise Satchel Paige. Then there are the films of all-star games and road trips that an owlish catcher named Quincy Trouppe took without ever thinking that they would be our lone celluloid link to the Negro leagues. And over everything loom the shadows of Josh Gibson and Jackie Robinson, the tragic figure who never made it to the white man's majors and the bold pioneer who did, both of them six feet under, both of them still larger than life. But it is Crutchfield who provides *Only the Ball Was White* with its balance of love and pain.

To him, baseball in any form was better than going down into the Missouri coal mines that swallowed his father. The game was a way of proving that even though he stood just 5-foot-8 and weighed but 140 pounds, he could rise as high as society's laws would let him. The bumpy rides on two-lane dirt roads, the ramshackle "colored" hotels, the 65-cents-a-day meal money – well, he just refused to worry about such things.

"When you're doing something you love to do," he says, "there's nothing lousy about it."

There is poetry in the way Crutchfield speaks about the game, poetry in the way he thinks about it. And the fact that he met his bride-to-be after making a breathtaking barehanded catch in the 1935 East-West Game is only part of the magic that consumes him.

Long ago he was thrilled to play in Pittsburgh in the company of Paige, Gibson, Cool Papa Bell, Judy Johnson, and Oscar Charleston – Hall of Famers all. And now he is thrilled to carry the autographs of Minnie Minoso and Elston Howard in his wallet, even though the men who signed them surely don't recognize him as one of their baseball forefathers. No harm done. Crutchfield remains at peace with his game, at least until he goes to sleep.

"I had a dream the other night," he says. "I dreamed I singled off a left-handed pitcher and the ball crossed over second base. I started running, but I couldn't get to first base. The ball crossed over the bag, but I couldn't get to first base."

The pity is that the dream was the only reality that Jimmie Crutchfield ever knew.

Chicago Sun-Times, March 9, 1980

4

Hit and Run   *Last of His Kind*

I'm not going out on any kind of limb when I say that we will never again see Bill Veeck's like as a team owner. What other member of his lodge would read enough books in a year to provide me with fodder for a Christmas gift list? While the big leagues were becoming the province of soulless corporations and fat cats with more money than brains or taste, Veeck remained a scuffler, laughing, spinning yarns, and scheming to keep the wolf from his door. Whether it was Chicago or Cleveland, he always did business the way he had the first time he opened shop, in what was then the minor league province of Milwaukee. Here I offer one visit with Veeck at Christmas and three glimpses of him at the end of a road that was never paved with gold, just the good times that lasted until he died in 1985.

. . . And Checking It Twice

Bill Veeck checked into Illinois Masonic Hospital the other day for
what he called "annual repairs." His hours away from the operating
room, he said, will be spent reading two novels – *True Confessions*,
a mystery that is more than a mystery by John Gregory Dunne, and
Union Dues, a slice of 1960s life by John Sayles. If Veeck likes them,
they may wind up under somebody's Christmas tree, for hc plans
to be home before December 25, and he has been known to give
books as gifts. In fact, nothing else would seem right coming from
Comiskey Park's resident literary critic.

When he is not renting a heavy hitter for the White Sox, infu-
riating baseball's bluenoses with his untraditional imagination, or
playing the courtly gentleman, Veeck can be found with book in
hand. He has consumed no fewer than 125 volumes on every subject
imaginable so far this year, a statistic that should make him the
salvation of last-minute shoppers. All they need are friends whose
taste for the printed word has not been obliterated by the urge to
watch reruns of *I Love Lucy*.

"The only hard-and-fast rule I have for selecting a book for someone," says Veeck, "is that it has to be a book I think has merit." His
wife, Mary Frances, who keeps up with him page for page, has tried
to refine that technique. "She is a genius at picking the book that
will delight someone," he says. "She also knows that sometimes you
have to give a book that will fit a person's image of himself rather
than one that might really shake him up and get him thinking."

You can see the effect Mary Frances has had on Veeck when he
talks about Stephen Birmingham's *Real Lace* and John R. Powers's

The Unoriginal Sinner and the Ice-Cream God. Both books are about Irish Catholics, both delighted Veeck, and yet both might offend people whose ethnic and religious sensibilities haven't been winterized. "I'd rather not step on any toes," Veeck says, never stopping to think how many shoeshines he has ruined for commissioner Bowie Kuhn.

The one book good enough to make Veeck forget about his conscience this Christmas is *Five Seasons,* the second collection of Roger Angell's baseball reportage from the *New Yorker.* "Maybe it's because I'm always trying to sell the game," says Veeck. Or maybe it is simply because he appreciates the wonderful things a skilled writer and observer can do with the English language. "Roger understands that some of the people in baseball are scufflers like me," he says, "and that some of the athletes are less than heroes. But he doesn't let it diminish his appreciation of the skill it takes to play. He selects the nuances that even people who watch the game every day overlook, and he makes them come to life with absolutely beautiful verbiage."

Sports books are not usually the unquenchable Veeck's glass of beer. Too many of them, he knows, are about the Mark Fidryches and Bruce Jenners of the world – cut-and-paste jobs intended to make a fast buck for an instant celebrity. The greed behind them, however, does not bother Veeck as much as the bad memories that come with books about Vietnam and Watergate. "Nobody on my gift list will get one," says the man who stood on the wooden leg World War II gave him and publicly opposed American involvement in Vietnam as early as 1965. "I don't like the idea of reliving nightmares."

On the other hand, he would love to see children enjoy the same early intellectual stimulation he had. But that will happen only if, like Veeck's father, parents are not afraid to mix gifts of toys and games with the works of Charles Dickens, Alexander Dumas, Mark Twain, Sir Arthur Conan Doyle, Jack London – great writers capable of helping the young realize that literature can take their minds farther than TV programmers can.

Even when he considers books for adults, Veeck relies on scenes from his youth. Consider his background for comparing *Ring*, by Jonathan Yardley, with *The Lardners*, by Ring Lardner Jr.: "I went to Amherst with Ring Lardner's kids. And we lived one floor below them on Kimbark, between 54th and 55th Streets, until both families got high class and moved out of the city." Given what he knows, Veeck prefers the Yardley book. "Ring Jr. relied too little on history," he says, "and too much on his feelings."

Which is not to say that Veeck ignores *his* feelings when selecting reading matter. Mary C. Nelson's *Maria Martinez* touched him because he knew the Pueblo Indian sculptor while he was attending high school in New Mexico 48 years ago and because she is now fighting to save her tribal heritage. Veeck is partial to *Six Men*, by Alistair Cooke, for two other personal reasons. The book makes him remember fondly the writing ability of Cooke, who now spends more time on TV, and it brings back to life two men he admired and whose flesh he once pressed – Humphrey Bogart and H. L. Mencken, Baltimore's uncommon scold.

"It's strange to spend so much time talking about nonfiction," Veeck says, "because, actually, I prefer reading fiction." And he has all sorts of suggestions about which of it ought to turn up on Christmas morning. For the Beowulfish, there is John Gardner's *October Light*. For thrill-seekers, there are John LeCarre's *The Honourable Schoolboy* and Robert Ludlum's *The Chancellor Manuscript*. For the gentle of heart, there are Colleen McCullough's *The Thorn Birds* and Iris Murdoch's *Henry and Cato*. And for those who would like to read about a character who has a lot of Veeck in him, there is *The Main*, by the perpetual best-seller Trevanian.

"The book is set on Main Street in Montreal, which is sort of like our West Madison Street," says Veeck. "It's about this old-time policeman who muscles people around and does other things his superiors don't like. He finds out he's dying – nobody else knows – and then he has to go out and solve a brutal murder. He does, and he does it his way. He's always a misfit."

Veeck seems bound and determined to leave baseball the same

way. He works toward that end even when doing something as frothy as putting together a list of gift books. "I think I have the perfect one for George Steinbrenner," he says. It is *Success*, by Michael Korda, who, like Yankee owner Steinbrenner, emphasizes business above humanity.

"Wait a minute," Veeck says. "I couldn't give it to Steinbrenner after all. It's in English."

Chicago Daily News, December 16, 1977

Prelude to Goodbye

Dawn was breaking over Baltimore, and in the half-light flickering through the newsroom's windows, the telephone on the reporter's desk looked cold and unpleasant. It was hardly a civilized hour to be calling anyone, but the city editor had other ideas. He wanted to know what Bill Veeck had to say about his ill-fated plan to buy the Orioles, and he wanted to know now. So the reporter dialed the phone and prepared to duck.

It would be three years and two cities later before he learned that dawn was Veeck's time, that the big "Halloo!" he heard was not the startled response of a deep sleeper whose pillow had just been pulled from under his head. When the phone rang on Maryland's Eastern Shore, Veeck had already been up for a good 45 minutes – drawing water to soak the stump of a leg lost in World War II, plowing through a small mountain of newspapers, and making sure a good book was within reach. Realizing none of that, the reporter asked his questions nervously and scarcely waited for the answers.

"I'm sorry about this, Mr. Veeck," he said as he began looking for an exit line. "I, uh, I just want to tell you how much I've enjoyed your books."

"Well, I thank you," Veeck said brightly. "And my children thank you."

Now it is our turn to thank him.

They are having Bill Veeck Night at Comiskey Park Tuesday, one big farewell before the arc lights go out on the White Sox' 66-year-old savior for what looks like the last time. Once the season is ended and the Sox are in the clutches of their new owners, there will be no more chances to watch him lob his empty beer mug to the waiting hospitality room bartender, no more chances to hear the *thump-thump-thump* of his wooden leg as he heads for seat 18 in the press box. His famous scoreboard may still explode, but he will be gone, and the rest of us will be poorer for it.

The temptation under the circumstances is to make a saint of the man, but even Veeck would laugh at the folly of that. If there ever was a halo over his head, it was obscured long ago by the fallout from drinking stories, too many cigarettes, and, yes, more dubious deals than one cares to acknowledge. Say what you will about the comings and goings of Bucky Dent, Richie Zisk, and Ron Blomberg, though: Veeck never claimed to be what he wasn't.

Just think back to late 1975, when this knight in battered armor was trying to scrape up the money to keep the White Sox from moving to Seattle. He was in the Continental Bank of Illinois building, talking some tightwad out of $500,000, and to make a point, he leaped to his feet. It was splendid theater and bad judgment. The next thing Veeck knew, he was face first on the floor amid the nuts, screws, and assorted thingamabobs from a wooden leg that had just come undone.

Very calmly, very quietly, he asked for a pair of pliers to reassemble himself.

"Bionic man I'm not," he said.

He was, rather, a beguiling mix of flesh and blood, a whimsical con man who could surprise you with what he couldn't do as well as with what he could. His old-fashioned instincts, for example, made it impossible for him to understand why women sportswriters clamored for access to clubhouses. But when he learned that his ballplayers were willing to let them in, Veeck simply opened the door like the gentleman he was.

Getting in the way was never his style. No doubt there are those who will dispute that, pointing to his Fourth of July scoreboard and his pinch-hitting midget and arguing that such is the handiwork of an egomaniac. What the detractors forget is that when the game started, Veeck dropped out of sight.

He wouldn't sit in a private box and scream at a struggling pitcher, à la George Steinbrenner of the Yankees. Nor would he drag politicians and celebrities around behind him like toy animals, à la Edward Bennett Williams of the Orioles. As soon as Veeck heard the first note of the National Anthem, he cared only for the same thing everyone else in Comiskey Park did – baseball.

There was something almost childlike about him as he watched a game unfold, a youthfulness that even the haze of cigarette smoke around his wrinkled visage couldn't obscure. He rooted for the White Sox with a charming innocence and applauded them, on those rare occasions when they deserved applause, with sweet sincerity. And always his eyes twinkled behind those hearing-aid glasses – twinkled with memories of his first go-round in Chicago, the happy days in Cleveland, and the crazy ones in St. Louis; twinkled with fond recollections of the drunks, fat men, and just plain wonderful people it had been his good fortune to call friends.

It seemed the only thing that Veeck liked more than the past was the future. The names of the kids in the Sox' farm system tripped lovingly off his tongue as he pictured them in the World Series he was building for and would never reach. They belonged to spring, the time of year when he was tan and brimming with hope. But reality was, alas, the way Veeck looked the summer night the Sox were sold. He had a team going nowhere, a boil on his pale neck, and a cough that would put him in the hospital two days later.

He was the picture of a loser, and yet he salvaged a victory. He had a daughter named Lisa who had come bearing a gift for "The Greatest Father in the World," and he had the names of three new books he wanted to recommend to the reporter who had called him from Baltimore long, long ago. Lisa smiled proudly and words, as usual, failed the reporter. "Come on," Bill Veeck said at last. "Let's go watch the game."

Chicago Sun-Times, September 28, 1980

Selling the Sox

The time and temperature sign said it was 7 degrees at 1:22 p.m., and the wind howling down the street called the sign a liar. It looked like the beginning of a memorable debate, but Bill Veeck, a rugged individualist without a topcoat, wasn't interested. He wasn't cold, either.

Cold doesn't fit Veeck's legend any more than ties, locks on office doors, or pictures of himself on his own walls. He is the antithesis of the frills-and-fancy-stuff ownership that plagues big league baseball these days, the last of the breed that survived by wit and guile instead of daddy's money. And if you were searching for a description of his appeal Tuesday as he waited for the traffic light to change, wearing only a summer-weight suit and refusing to shiver, the words came from the hosannas of passing cabbies.

Nary a one in the daily parade didn't slow down at the sight of Veeck out on Monroe and Franklin Streets, leaning into the wind, trying to stay upright on his wooden leg. Some honked their horns, others shouted their good will, but only Samuel Spatafora took the initiative to stop and ask the question of the hour: "Hey, Bill, whatta you gonna do now?"

"Be a bum!" Veeck shouted back.

And the wind carried their laughter away.

It was over at last. The White Sox belonged to somebody else – not the people Veeck had in mind three months ago, of course, but $20 million could make the Hunchback of Notre Dame look good. So for the previous 3 1/2 hours on the 72nd floor of the Sears Tower, Veeck had been left-handing his name on one document after another, watching small clauses be retyped and listening to heavyweight lawyers for both sides call the bank to make sure the check had cleared.

He used the same pen he had dragged out of his pocket when he bought the Sox five years ago. To the mystification of those who best know his distaste for convention, he even found some keys to hand over to Jerry Reinsdorf, one of the new principal owners. Nothing was going to go awry if Veeck could help it. "I've been unemployed before," he said, "but I've never worked so hard to do it."

When Veeck sold the Cleveland Indians in 1950, it was because his first wife wanted out and wanted her money too. "She and her attorney decided they'd better get it while there was some," he said. When he sold the St. Louis Browns in 1953, it was because his partners low-balled him instead of joining him in a court battle to move the team to Baltimore. "Needless to say," he said, "they weren't invited back on any of our later deals." When he sold the White Sox for the first time, in 1961, he thought he might have to change "deals" to the singular. "The Mayo Brothers told me I was dying," he said, "and I had every reason to believe them."

In light of that, Veeck's return to Chicago in 1976 deserved to have been triumphant. That it wasn't was just another of life's bad jokes. There were dreary ball clubs and floods in the outfield, and who will ever forget the rack and ruin of Disco Demolition Night? The only thing more disheartening was the way commissioner Bowie Kuhn and the American League's other owners repaid him with venom for keeping their product in Chicago. They hadn't wanted him back in the first place, and when they couldn't stop him, they made good and sure he suffered as he looked for the exit. They sabotaged his deal with Edward J. DeBartolo, the Ohio-based shopping mall baron, and forced him to sell to a group that boasts of its class and comes on as though the previous tenant had turned Comiskey Park into a mausoleum.

"I think my fellow owners are probably all out celebrating right now, getting stoned," Veeck said Tuesday. "And I'm sure they never want to see me again. They probably wish I'd take up beekeeping in Peru or Argentina or wherever those killer bees are."

It was the bitter end, but 66-year-old Bill Veeck was laughing. Looking back on his career as baseball's reigning Barnum, with his pinch-hitting midgets and exploding scoreboards, there was really no other way he could leave. Sadness was for another time, another place. He was going to meet his wife, Mary Frances, for lunch now, so they could talk about the subject they left untouched during the hard going just past. "I plan to ask her about the future," he said, "and she's probably going to tell me to have a couple more cans of beer."

Veeck laughed again and looked out the window of the car that was carrying him up Jackson Street, watching the sidewalks for strangers whose lives he might have brightened, searching his mind for the reason behind his delightful lack of despair. He had just walked away from his toughest go in half a century of hustling, and he felt better for it. From general manager Roland Hemond to the lowliest member of the grounds crew, there had been no breaking of the White Sox' ranks. They had suffered together, endured together, grown stronger together. The result was something special.

"Let me tell you a story," Veeck said as the car turned north on Lake Shore Drive. "One of the last visitors we had at the park was Al Szabo, a photographer from *Inside Sports*, the new magazine. He came out one day and took a lot of pictures, and then we sat around drinking beer and telling stories. The next day he came back, and we drank some more beer and told some more stories. And the day after that, there he was again. He knew he had to leave, but you know what he said? He said, 'There aren't enough places like this anymore.'"

It was 7 degrees, the wind chill made it more like 19 below, and Bill Veeck didn't need a coat.

Chicago Sun-Times, February 4, 1981

To the Bleachers Once More

He sits beneath the last manually operated scoreboard in the big leagues, the one he helped bolt together back in '37, when he was young and the Cubs were the light of his life. They were his father's team, and they played in a park that, at this writing, has yet to acknowledge the existence of the incandescent bulb, but they were still capable of bowing to the kind of progress you can treasure. When the order came down to erect Wrigley Field's bleachers, the same free spirit who holds court there now could be found amid the brick and mortar.

"I didn't build everything," Bill Veeck takes care to point out, "but I built quite enough of it, thank you." Before he could lean back and admire his masterpiece, however, he had to plant the ivy that still adorns the outfield walls, because P. K. Wrigley just assumed it would be there. The reclusive gum baron was bringing some friends to the park not to root for the team he owned then, but to admire the foliage that wasn't even planted until Veeck had worked all night. When the impromptu landscaper was finished, he had the same overwhelming need he does 45 years after the fact.

"Beer!" he rumbles thirstily. "Oh, beer man!"

And the race among the vendors is on.

All of them recognize Veeck's beautifully craggy face, and some of them even know the man himself. The old-timers reminisce about the days when Jack Ruby was hustling toy birds outside the park, not writing history with a pistol. The kids pass on good wishes from their aunts and uncles, and after seeing Veeck in the center-field seats 20 times this season, they also wonder why he hasn't visited the South Side and the White Sox, the last team he called his own.

"They wouldn't let me drink my beer there," he says, his eyes reflecting the smile that the foam on his lips is hiding. "I couldn't be at home in such a class operation as they're operating there. The new owner, Fast Eddie – that is his name, isn't it? – is such a professional that he doesn't want me and my kind of people spilling beer on the furniture."

For the first time since Veeck sold the Sox to Eddie Einhorn and Jerry Reinsdorf a year and a half ago, there is every indication that the furniture wouldn't be the only thing in danger. He has listened to Einhorn alternately praise him with faint damns and treat him like a worthless brother-in-law who finally has taken the hint and moved on. But he kept his peace until the reconstructed Sox started playing now-you-have-it, now-you-don't with Ron Schueler's job as their pitching coach. Schueler was part of Veeck's Comiskey Park family, and even though he was promoted to assistant general manager after the mind games were over, his old boss is still boiling. "If that's a class operation," he says, "I guess it's time I spoke out."

"You haven't done that before, you know," someone says.

"Oh, but I'll do it again."

The promise is one that might endear Veeck to the Cubs' recently enshrined brain trust. It should not, however, be the only thing. Team president Andy McKenna and general manager Dallas Green should realize that, even at 68, Veeck represents the spirit of Wrigley Field's bleachers.

He wears as little as modesty allows – a pair of khaki shorts seems to be the staple of his wardrobe – and the sun has turned him a deeper brown than his artificial leg ever was. He can joke about using most of his suntan lotion to protect a head that features more skin than hair, and he shares the stuff with any bleacherite who isn't afraid of smelling like a piña colada. He helps strangers with crossword puzzles, buys beer for visiting TV anchor ladies, cuts up with erstwhile minor leaguers and football executives alike, and pays enough attention to the games to realize what's what with the Cubs. He calls Ryne Sandberg, their splendid rookie, "Mr. Sandberg," and when Keith Moreland, their vagabond slugger, crashes into the left-field wall, he points out that it's the wall that should be checked for damage.

Indeed, if the Cubs were interested in reflecting baseball's true charm instead of hard-nosing their way to success, they would enlist Veeck as their ambassador to Wrigley's distant reaches. Job or no, however, he is going to be out there beguiling everybody around him just by seeking what he always has at ball games – fun.

"You know, I got a call from Reggie Jackson the other day," he says. "Oh, I think Reggie is a wonderful ballplayer. You put him up there with two on and two out in the ninth inning and it's like giving Popeye a can of spinach. Well, Reggie wanted me to write to his daddy, Martinez – Martinez Jackson, who's a tailor in Philadelphia. He had a hip transplant. So I wrote and said, 'I'm sorry to hear about it, but I must welcome you to the group. And it isn't as bad as you think. Your son has done quite well without being able to run much, either.'"

The laughter that greets Veeck's story loosens a memory about another slugger, a fellow with fewer accomplishments than Jackson but a decidedly more historic name. "When my daddy was running the Cubs," Veeck says, "he wired one of his scouts to sign George Washington in Dallas. Right away the scout wired back, 'Will do. And on my way home I'll stop in Springfield and sign Abe Lincoln.'"

Before Veeck can spin another yarn, he is stopped by a hand on his bare shoulder. The hand belongs to a kid in a Black Hawks jersey who has decided that the White Sox' sleek new uniforms aren't doing much for Greg Luzinski's sumo wrestler physique.

"Now I know why you had those guys wearing their shirts outside their pants when you owned the Sox," the kid tells Veeck. "You didn't want people to know how fat Luzinski is."

Veeck smiles as if he and the kid are the only people in the world who understand the ploy. "I could become very fond of you," he says.

The feeling, of course, is mutual.

Chicago Sun-Times, July 25, 1982

5

Twilight of the Long-ball Gods

Lord, how they hated to see Moe Hill come to Waterloo. When he had a bat in his hands and a Wisconsin Rapids uniform on his back, a sense of dread rose from those Iowa townies like summer heat off two-lane blacktop.

They would have loved to know that Moe considered rickety Municipal Stadium an affront to personal hygiene because the visitors' clubhouse had only one shower. As it was, though, Waterloo's paying customers thought they had to get under his skin by their lonesome. The moment the Wisconsin Rapids team bus pulled up outside the park, there was an antiquated black gent who wouldn't stop yelling and pounding his cane until Moe came over, all shy smiles and humility. Not that anybody else in the crowd bought his act, you understand. They burned his ears with standing ovations when he struck out and fanned the flames by waving placards that said YOU CAN'T MAKE A MOUNTAIN OUT OF MOE HILL. It seemed like an awful lot of fuss over a game in the backwaters of baseball and a slugger who was stuck there, always bidding bon voyage to kids bound for the big leagues. But the stranger who dared say so received a hasty lesson in the stuff legends are made of.

"See that cemetery out there?" some old boy in a buck-and-a-quarter grandstand seat would ask.

And his eyes would sweep out to left center field, beyond the wooden fence and its sun-bleached ads, up a gentle hill, and into a cluster of headstones and memorial bouquets. A good 550 feet as the home run flies.

"That's where Moe Hill hit one."

§ The bushes used to be full of heroes with no future – cleanup hitters who had washed out of the majors or, as in Moe Hill's case, never got closer than a newspaper campaign in Minneapolis. Some of them played because they didn't want to do anything else, others because they couldn't, and there was always a club somewhere between Meridian, Mississippi, and Missoula, Montana, that had a place for them. In those outposts, what got people's engines running was the damage a big lug could do against pitchers who were either scared kids or tired old men. Hell, home runs put people in the seats.

Of course, there were more seats down in the minors in those days – 59 leagues in 1949 and 48 teams in North Carolina alone. Baseball's ladder went all the way down to Class D then, which makes today's Class A and rookie-league operations sound as effete as they really are. Rookie league? Listen, those were men who used to provide small town America with its long-ball electricity. Though they may have had failings with blubber, booze, or breaking pitches, it didn't matter when there wasn't a television set in the den to bring you Mike Schmidt and Reggie Jackson in living color. In the happy times before the minors shrunk to their present 17 leagues, vagabond sluggers feared neither a deadline for making it to the majors nor, if they failed, exile to slow pitch softball. As long as they could get around on the fast one, they knew there would be somebody who thought they could bring a pennant to Bushville and a smile to the paying customers' faces. Even in Hollywood, home runs could make people forget about Jayne Mansfield.

She was the mascot of a local Pacific Coast League entry called the Stars – what else? – and most years her measurements outshone everyone's power production. But in 1957 pompadoured Dick Stuart blew into Hollywood on the wind of the 66 homers he had hit in Lincoln, Nebraska, the summer before. When he cracked five in his first four games with the Stars, he found himself posing for a picture with La Mansfield and having his fancy tickled by a question he must have been waiting for all his life.

"How come you're getting the headlines and I'm not?" sweet Jayne whispered in his ear.

"Because I'm hitting the long ball," Stuart chirped.

He was not alone. On the other side of town, Steve Bilko was hitting 111 home runs in two seasons for the Los Angeles Angels and turning a dowdy crackerbox called Wrigley Field into his personal Versailles. Bilko's heroics wore out the imaginations of L.A. sportswriters – they stalled after dreaming up "Stout Steve" and "the Slugging Seraph" – but that was nothing compared to the consternation caused by his avoirdupois. With all the hullabaloo about getting him on a scale, you would have thought nobody cared about why he had gone belly up with the Cardinals and the Cubs. "Not Even Mrs. Bilko Knows His Weight," a headline in the *Los Angeles Times* proclaimed.

Maybe it was just as well. She might have been harder on Bilko than he already was on himself. After a night of drinking the beer he loved so much, he would retreat to the bathroom, lock the door, pad the cracks around it with towels, and turn the place into a steam room. The effort, alas, was hardly worth the result. He was still fat.

It was like that with Bilko and his brethren: there always seemed to be a chink in their armor. With Buzz Arlett, who hit as many as 54 homers and batted as high as .382 during 19 seasons in Triple A, the problem was that fly balls never landed in his glove, just on his head. Nick Cullop once bashed 54 homers for the old Minneapolis Millers, but too often he dragged his bat back to the dugout moaning about "that old hipper-dipper," the dread curveball. Minneapolis, it seems, was fertile ground for sluggers with a way with words. To celebrate his 69 homers there in 1933, Joe Hauser has spent every day since describing them to anyone who will listen. George Wilson, who dragged a snazzy batting average into town two decades later, compared himself to Ted Williams. "He wanted us to call him 'the Thumper,'" Kansas City manager Jim Frey says. "We laughed like hell over that, but George didn't care. He just kept telling everybody he could hit buckshot with barbed wire."

South of the border, Al Pinkston never said much. Most likely it was for fear of letting it slip that he'd lied nine years off his age when he enlisted in the Philadelphia A's farm system. Pinkston's deceit was a sign of the times, not of his own moral bankruptcy. World War II and baseball's color line had kept him from where he should have been, and when Farnham, Quebec, of the Provincial League finally beckoned in 1951, he couldn't help himself. Besides, it was never any secret that he had some miles on him. His feet always hurt. Even when he was hanging around the hotel lobby in a suit and tie during the Caribbean World Series, he wore house slippers. Those aching feet never stopped Pinkston from pounding line drives, though. The worst season he had in the Mexican League was 1965, the last of the seven he played there. He batted .345, 27 points beneath his career average with Veracruz and the Mexico City Reds, but there was a reasonable explanation for such a sub-par performance: Pinkston, twice a grandfather, was 47 years old.

Maybe the infamous Mexican water preserved him. It certainly hasn't hurt Hector Espino, at 42 still polishing his reputation as the Hispanic Babe Ruth. Nobody in baseball's outback has ever matched his 450-plus home runs, but to show what a regular fellow he is, Espino has never lost his appreciation for the peso. "Down in winter ball in '69, Hector and me was in a home-run hitting contest," says Roger Freed, another slugger who has taken his share of bus rides, "and he comes up to me before we start swinging and says, 'No matter who wins, let's split the prize money.'"

It was just what you would expect from someone who has earned minor league pay throughout his career, yet Espino could have done better. "When I was with the California Angels, we invited him to spring training one year," White Sox general manager Roland Hemond says. "He was a big league hitter who wasn't being tested. Good compact swing. Everything we wanted. And he never showed up. Never even called us."

The cold shoulder made Espino an anomaly, for classic minor league sluggers are supposed to be like Moe Hill. They are supposed to yearn for a shot at the big show and swear they have been done wrong when they don't get it.

"I thought I was good at what I done," Moe says. "I hit all those home runs and drove in all those runs, and the Twins kept sending me back to the same place. The only thing that kept me going was a love of the game. Well, maybe I did do a little dreaming, too. I always thought I could hit major league pitching."

He swallows hard and looks around to make sure none of the Kansas City farmhands he coaches are listening.

"Still do," he says softly.

But the only people likely to believe Moe Hill are those who saw him leave his calling card throughout the Midwest League – in Wausau, Wisconsin, where the wind always blew out; and Danville, Illinois, where the lack of a clubhouse meant you had to take turns dressing under the grandstand; and all the other towns where dinner for a ballplayer was a hot dog and a Coke. Only one dot on the map could truly claim Moe as its adopted son, though, and that was Wisconsin Rapids. By the time he took his last toehold there, he was bigger than Consolidated Water Power and Papers, and Consolidated owned the whole damn town.

Nobody figured anything like that would happen when Moe showed up to play first base for the last 20 games of 1971. He was nothing more than Class A flotsam, working on his third team of the season and trying to prove that the Baltimore Orioles had been wrong in releasing him two years earlier. It's hard to say what happened after that. "I always tried to give it my best shot, you know," Moe says, and suddenly his best shots were shaping the Midwest League in his own image. He won the triple crown in '74 and the home run championship for four straight years, set a league record for homers with 41 in '77 and made everybody forget that Sal Bando, Gorman Thomas, and a host of other 1,000-watt names had passed this way.

The pitchers who didn't like it threw at Moe's head, but his response was as foursquare as his statistics. "Fighting never did no good," he says. "Just gets you hurt or kicked out of the game." So he would dust himself off and go downtown where there was no downtown. "The one time I saw Moe do that," says Ted Wirtz Jr., the Wisconsin Rapids mailman who was his best friend, "the ball was still going up when it left the park."

This wasn't some hero imprisoned by a television screen, either. Moe Hill was right there, throwing out the first ball at the Little League opener and pedaling his bike around town with an army of admiring kids in his wake. They were the same kids who hung over the dugout roof at Witter Field and offered him bubblegum for base hits or, better yet, his autograph. "I'll bet some of those kids have my name scribbled on 100 different pieces of paper," Moe says. In their own way, the town's adults adored him just as much. "One year they told me I'd gotten 300 write-in votes for mayor," he says. "I never looked it up, though." It was enough to have bank officials calling him by his first name, his landlady giving him a venison roast at the end of every season, and nobody saying anything about his being the town's lone black. Color didn't matter; home runs did. When Wisconsin Rapids played its 1977 finale, the good burghers gave Moe a plaque, a gold pen, and, just as he was about to say thanks, a six-foot-long bat that a lot of pitchers must have thought he'd been using all along.

You can imagine the feelings of pride and admiration and maybe even love that swept over the people in the stands that day. They had come to salute the man who gave them seven summers to remember. What they may not have realized as they smiled down on Moe Hill was that he was the last of a breed.

§ "It was nothing to pick up an afternoon paper and see my name in a headline on the front page. I don't think they even do that anymore."

The thought pleases Howitzer Howie Moss. He sells Buicks for a living now, but part of him will always be swinging from the heels. After the original Orioles stole out of Baltimore and before Brooks Robinson arrived half a century later to usher in the present era of big-time excellence, Howitzer Howie made the city forget that it was stuck in the International League. Fifty-three homers in 1947 did the trick so well that when the Orioles unloaded his $6,000-a-year contract one season later, Rodger Pippen, the sports editor of the *News-Post*, ran general manager Tommy Thomas out of town.

But that's another story. Just like the one about how pie-faced Howie got malaria playing in the Cotton States League. Just like the one about how he played outlaw ball in North Carolina for four years after that. Just like the one about how he genuflected before Judge Landis to get back on the right side of the tracks and damn near took Mel Ott's place in right field in the Polo Grounds.

The story we're interested in began when Howitzer Howie retired in 1943, after enduring too many bush league lumps. Thomas tracked him down at the Hoboken, New Jersey, shipyard where he was working and tempted him with a left-field fence in old Oriole Park that was 290 feet from the plate. "I told Tommy I'd sign right there," Howie says. His arrival meant a pennant in '44, a series of memorable slugging duels with Hank Sauer of Syracuse, and an image that bettors and bookmakers would never forget. "They called me Howitzer Howie for the shots I hit. The fans got to expect home runs all the time."

For every other Oriole, the odds on hitting one were 20–1; for him, they were 7–1. "That's what the gamblers told me," he says. But he could have figured that out for himself after he hit five doubles and no homers in a Sunday doubleheader.

"You know what the fans did?" Howitzer Howie says. "They booed me."

§ The barmaid was just a little bit of a thing, so she couldn't really knock Red Howell out until help came. Her only hope was to keep stunning him as she sat astride his chest at three in the morning and walloped him with a full bottle of Scotch.

"Poor Murray," Bill Veeck says, careful to use the name Howell's mother gave him even when recalling such a revolting development. "By the time I got there, he had 30 lumps on his head."

It was 1942 and Veeck, a second-year owner instead of the legendary wreck he is now, was staring at the red-dirt Georgia farm boy he had hired to be the linchpin of the Milwaukee Brewers' batting order. On paper Howell looked like he would be the scourge of the American Association. Just two seasons before, in Baltimore, he had batted .359 with 29 homers and 122 RBIs. But on the floor of the Sunset Café in Ocala, Florida, after losing a spring training row with a barmaid, he looked more like a load of dirty wash.

"He had his problems drinking, Murray did," Veeck says. The biggest one was that bartenders always wanted to stop serving Howell after he was stewed to the gills. To hurdle this barrier, he enlisted the aid of the teenaged bride who accompanied him to Milwaukee. She carried a tiny pearl-handled pistol in her purse, and when a request for a refill was turned down, she would hand the heater to Howell, and he would convince whoever was behind the bar that the customer was always right. "I suppose the idea had its merits," Veeck says, "but after opening day Murray went out to celebrate his four hits" – the record book says 0-for-2, but whose story is this? – "and he ran into a most disputatious bartender. Naturally, Murray used the one call the police gave him to wake me up at 3 a.m."

Justice in Milwaukee worked 24 hours a day, which led Veeck and the Brewers' manager, Jolly Cholly Grimm, to believe they could get Howell out of night court before sunup. They walked their slugger back and forth in a corridor until he appeared ready for action, then told him to put on an apologetic face.

"Young man," the judge intoned, "are you aware of the charges against you?"

"You son of a bitch," Howell growled. "You're trying to frame me."

A hasty exit. More walking. More counseling from Veeck and Grimm. Then back in court.

"Now," the judge said, "do you know who I am?"

"Yeah," Howell said. "You're the son of a bitch who's trying to frame me."

The answer won him an order to be out of town by sundown. When Veeck telephoned the judge to say Howell was on a bus to Knoxville of the Southern Association, he did it, appropriately enough, from a saloon.

§ Gene Asher can still tell you the starting lineup for the 1941 Atlanta Crackers, "probably the greatest Atlanta team of all time." He is 53 years old, the founder of his own insurance agency, and a colonel in the Marine Corps Reserves, but some things never change. Even after he had assumed the trappings of adulthood, he couldn't see a certain salesman in Rich's Department Store without shouting, "Number 3, Charlie Glock, third base!" And when Glock died last winter, Asher went to his funeral and bawled like a baby.

They were friends – a slugger and a kid, a hero and a hero-worshipper. In an age when men who bat .320 and drive in 115 runs are as remote as heads of state, that may be hard to understand. But try to imagine the way Atlanta was when Ponce de Leon Park – "Poncey" to the natives – was standing, with the streetcar stopping in front of it and train tracks running behind the right-field fence. It was as intimate a ballpark as ever held 14,000 people, and the pin-striped Crackers, even though they were boldly billed as "the Yankees of the Minor Leagues," seemed to know all the regulars by their first names. Gene Asher became a regular because he was a vendor, and when Charlie Glock found out the kid was crazy about him, he invited him onto the field to play pepper.

Asher walked the way his hero did, pigeon-toed, with his arms swinging wide. When he played softball, he rested his bat on his shoulder the way Glock did. "But I still popped up all the time," he says. He even wrote a poem that wound up on the editorial page of the *Atlanta Journal*: "No doubt you've heard of Charlie Glock / He hits the ball as hard as a rock. . . ." Asher's friends called him "Charlie Boy," but he didn't mind. After games the great Glock used to treat him to fried chicken at the White Dot Grill, and one Sunday Asher got to take his hero home for dinner.

"My family lived in a courtyard apartment then," he says, "and all the other tenants were Cracker fans too. In those days, everybody was. Anyway, I kept telling 'em, 'Charlie's coming, Charlie's coming,' but I'm not sure they believed me until the doubleheader was over and we walked into the court. They were all sitting out on their front steps waiting to see what was going to happen, and as soon as they saw Charlie, they couldn't help themselves. They started applauding."

§ When the hitters got through with the West Texas–New Mexico League in 1948, it looked like a cabbage patch after an invasion of rabbits. There were four hitters batting over .400, and 35 of the league's 64 regulars topped .300, but that really isn't anything until you hear what Bob Crues did. The tall, bald center fielder of the Amarillo Gold Sox made people forget about his .404 batting average and 69 homers by piling up 254 RBIs in 140 games. Think about that for a minute: 254 RBIs should be two seasons' work. Then again, maybe they were just proof of how few curveballs got thrown in those arid parts.

"When you had 60 minor leagues or whatever it was," Jim Frey says, "a lot of people thought they could call themselves pitchers."

The higher a hitter went, though, the less he saw of those soft touches and the more he saw of his maker. "Uncle Charlie give 'em fits," Frey says. Uncle Charlie is code for the curve, the pitch that Steve Bilko supposedly never mastered and that the Twins used as a reason for keeping Moe Hill in exile. "They never said I couldn't hit a fastball," Moe says in self-defense. Certainly not. That wouldn't have fit the cliché of the career minor league slugger, the strong man who couldn't deal with finesse. But the truth is, that image helped a lot of heavy hitters hang pitchers up to dry.

"Those second-guessers were so busy yakking about how I couldn't handle the curve that they never saw what I was hitting my home runs off," Howitzer Howie Moss says. "A good fastball was what got me out. It gets all of 'em out. But, boy, when they threw a curveball, they had to let up, and that was just my speed."

Only one other free swinger was ever so blunt about what he could and couldn't hit, and you have to go back to the 1920s to find him. John King, the owner of the sweetest southpaw stroke the East Texas League ever saw, couldn't have connected against a left-hander if the left-hander had run across the plate carrying the ball. Understandably, this shortcoming prevented King from rising to the majors. He responded by despising lefties of every persuasion, even the blind street fiddler he once gave a silver dollar. When he saw what hand the fiddler held his bow with, King took his money back.

His foul mood lasted long after he stopped batting .330 and started drilling oil. Indeed, he went so far as to turn his back on Lubbock, Texas, where he'd made his millions. The reason, he said, should have been self-explanatory: "Too many left-handed neighbors."

§ If you judge strictly by home runs, there has never been a summer that was the equal of the one Roswell, New Mexico, had back in '54. Long, tall Joe Bauman bashed 72 for the hometown Rockets, a record that still stands, and by the time he'd finished, he was as much of a national celebrity as the Class C Longhorn League ever produced. [Author's note: Obviously Barry Bonds has since rendered the preceding sentence inaccurate.] The boys from *Life* and *Sports Illustrated* even came down to take his picture when he hit three homers on the last day of the season. The problem was, all the people around the country who'd been reading one-inch wire service stories about Bauman suddenly discovered that he wasn't a kid first baseman they were going to be seeing a lot of in the future.

He was 32 that season, and the only reason he was playing was that an aspiring bush league mogul had found him pumping gas three years earlier. "I told him I didn't think my contract with the Boston Braves was worth my jockey strap," he says, "but if he was crazy enough to buy it, go ahead." The mini-mogul did, ignoring the fact that Bauman had already quit pro ball twice, once to join the navy, once to play semipro for the Elk City, Oklahoma, Elks. "What the hell," Bauman says, "they paid me as much as I was getting in the Eastern League."

So he returned with his eyes wide open, not terribly impressed by a Roswell team bus that had Pullman beds and realizing that "three out of four days I hit against piss-poor pitchers." It was a job, that's all. "I went to Roswell looking for a place to settle down," he says. "I was playing my way out of the damn game."

That isn't a very romantic picture, but once Bauman had circled the bases, shaken his teammates' hands, and read the morning papers, he didn't have much to look forward to, especially on payday. Oh, there was all that talk about how Steve Bilko was the third best-paid first baseman in the game, even though the Coast League was his home. And Howitzer Howie Moss will tell you, "One year I made as much under the table as over it." But they were the exceptions, and Joe Bauman was the rule.

"I made $4,000 the year I hit 72 homers," he says, "and I made $4,000 the year after." Two decades later, Moe Hill had to settle for $400 less than that. "I never got paid for what I did," he says. Maybe the only way he would have is if he had played in Amarillo when Bob Crues did.

"They were crazy about baseball out here after the war was over," says Billie Crues, Bob's wife for 39 years and his mouthpiece since he had a stroke in 1974. "They closed the stores when the ballgames were on, and that old park was packed. The people loved Bob. He wasn't making but $4,000-a-year salary, but some nights he'd bring home five or six hundred dollars that the crowd gave him. There was a wire fence back of home plate, and they'd just keep shoving dollar bills at him. One businessman – he's dead now – even tore a $100 bill in two and gave Bob one half for a homer one night and the other half for a homer the next."

The gesture was a splendid mixture of the exotic and the practical, but lest you think Amarillo had a patent on such things, let us recall Colorado Springs in 1951. There was a steakhouse in that Western League whistle-stop that awarded its specialty for every home run hit by the Sky Sox. Obviously, the proprietors weren't counting on the arrival of Fat Pat Seerey, a failed big leaguer whose appetite was equaled only by his capacity for the long ball. Fat Pat hit 44 homers and left the enterprising restaurateurs with a dilemma they had only one way to solve.

On the last day of the season, they presented him with a cow.

§ You understand just how long ago it all happened when roll is called. Steve Bilko died three winters ago with hardly anyone remembering that he hit the last home run in L.A.'s Wrigley Field. Cancer tracked Al Pinkston down at his stevedore's job in New Orleans this year. Bob Crues's stroke hit him so hard he won't even go to the Panhandle Sports Hall of Fame's annual dinner.

Whether that makes Joe Bauman the lucky one is up to you to decide. He sells beer for a living in Roswell, and every now and again business takes him out past the ballpark where he made his name. They don't have baseball there anymore, though. Just rodeos.

It's even worse in Atlanta, where Ponce de Leon Park was leveled for a shopping center. What the wrecking crews couldn't destroy, of course, were the memories of the men who played there. Bob Montag, the ritziest of Crackers, still gets recognized 23 years after his last game. People don't care that the home run he hit for his club record of 39 was a foul ball; they just know what Der Tag could do and want to see more, which is why he got to hit the first homer at Atlanta-Fulton County Stadium. The Braves didn't suit him up or anything sentimental like that. Shoot, he hadn't been in a uniform for seven seasons when the opportunity arose. But he was out there filming a commercial for a savings and loan before the new park opened in 1965, and somebody asked him if he wanted to take a few cuts.

"The second ball I hit wound up in the blue seats in right field," Montag says. "Boy, I damn near passed out."

Then perhaps he can understand how the Fort Myers Royals felt when they watched Moe Hill take his final swings in anger. The Royals had heard of Moe – who in the bushes hadn't? – but they thought he would never do anything in the Florida State League last year except jerk an occasional ball over the fence in batting practice. After all, he was their hitting coach. But when injuries wracked the Royals, Moe was called to action in the dirty, dimly lit outhouse that serves as the Key West ballpark.

"First time up, he hit a home run," Royals general manager Dave Brunk says.

Moe smiles at his boss's memory. "Actually," he says, "I walked twice first."

It was like old times. Moe hit another homer, this one to win a game, and he had his average up to .340 before he sat down for keeps at 33. "Sure, I would have liked to keep playing him," manager Brian Murphy says, "but my bosses in Kansas City weren't having any of it." It's a kid's game now. You make it in five or six years, or you go home, get a job as an accountant, and play slow-pitch softball. A guy like Moe Hill, a guy who invested 14 years of his life in baseball and got nothing in return, can only wonder what happened.

One year after his legend came to life for the last time, he stops on the top step of the Fort Myers dugout and listens to a familiar sound. The Royals are trailing Lakeland 2–1 going into the bottom of the ninth, and from a row of old-timers sitting behind home plate, there comes a woman's voice: "We want Moe! We want Moe!"

He doesn't even glance at her, just trots to the first-base coach's box, but the woman continues her chant.

"We want Moe! We want Moe!"

When he finally turns around, she can see him smiling.

Inside Sports, August 31, 1981

6

The Wild, Wild Past

The paper would say Tommy's going to pitch tonight. Hell, I pitched every night.
Give me six runs and I'd beat anybody. I was the Mitch Williams of my time.
– *Tom Brookshier*

To Philadelphians of a certain age, he will always be at cornerback
for the Eagles, a tough little mutt who would dent your fenders if
you caught a pass in front of him and buy you a drink afterward to
prove it wasn't anything personal. But for four weeks in the spring
of 1954, he belonged to Roswell, New Mexico, the town where he
was born, and to a baseball team called the Rockets because the
scientists out on the nearby desert were poking holes in the sky with
their experiments.

And the amazing thing is, Tom Brookshier wasn't the biggest
name in the Class C Longhorn League, one step from the bottom
of pro ball, a category and a league that have long since vanished.
Here was a man who had just spent his rookie season in the NFL
shoulder to shoulder with Eagle legends Chuck Bednarik and Pete
Pihos, and he wasn't even the biggest name on the Rockets. That
distinction belonged to the tall drink of water who spent road trips
sleeping on a bunk in the back of the team's red, white and blue bus
while Brookshier had to sit up telling jokes to a Cuban shortstop
who didn't speak English.

Joe Bauman got the bunk because he was on his way to hitting
72 home runs that year, and no one in the annals of baseball for pay
has ever matched his feat. [Author's note: See Barry Bonds once
again.] You may laugh at the thought of a guy named Joe holding

a record you didn't know existed, but to the Sweetwater Spudders and the Carlsbad Potashers and all the other teams he belabored in the far reaches of Texas and New Mexico, he was Babe Ruth, Roger Maris and Hank Aaron rolled into one. If there were ever any suspicions that Bauman was the figment of some wire-service stringer's imagination, *Life* magazine ended them by dispatching a photographer to take his picture. You could look it up. Or you could listen to Brookshier, 62 and retired from talking sports on WIP, recall the night he saw one of Bauman's homers stop a rodeo cold.

"The rodeo grounds were next to where we played in Roswell," he says, "but there wasn't any connecting them before Joe came along. He got a low, inside fastball one night, and when he hit it, it looked like the second baseman was going to make the catch. But the ball kept rising. It was still going up when it cleared the fence, and it didn't stop until it landed in the middle of the damn rodeo. Must have traveled 550 feet. Well, those cowboys didn't know what the hell had happened at first. Then they forgot all about the rodeo, and they took off their hats and whooped and hollered for Joe."

This was baseball when it had a soul, when it was played for a few bucks and a lot of laughs by men who had survived World War II and the Depression. There were only 16 teams in the major leagues then, but the minors had upwards of 300, employing journeymen and dreamers who could tolerate dim lights and lumpy fields and the lonesome wail of a freight train on the other side of the outfield wall. It was as though the players in America's bush league outposts had made their own pact with the devil: They would trade the all-night bus rides they were always taking for a chance to draw a paycheck that said they were pros.

If it weren't for the Phillies, there wouldn't be a team in baseball today that could make you think such passion still exists. John Kruk, Dave Hollins, Lenny Dykstra – you bet they would have loved the Longhorn League. But how many others from their generation would have felt the same? Baltimore's Cal Ripken Jr., certainly. And Kirby Puckett from Minnesota. After that, however, the list starts thinning out, which is a shame not because of what it says about the new breed, but because of what they would have missed if they'd passed up the good old days with a right-handed pitcher named Brookshier.

"I had a hell of a great time," he says on the 40th anniversary of his tour as a Roswell Rocket. "That was as much fun as I ever had playing anything." And this, remember, comes from someone who helped the Eagles win their last NFL championship, someone who is only too happy to reminisce about that December afternoon in 1960 when they iced Green Bay at raucous Franklin Field.

But six years earlier, after proving he could hold his own in Philly, Brookshier wasn't banking on a glorious future, for Uncle Sam owned his hindquarters. He told the Eagles' management that he would be wearing an Air Force uniform for the next two years because of the ROTC commitment he had made at Colorado University, and then reported for duty in Washington, D.C. "I stayed a week before they told me to go home," he says. "The goddamn Air Force didn't know who I was."

There was no guessing how long the confusion would last, which was a curse as well as a blessing. Brookshier loved being a civilian, but he loved making money, too, and none was in sight now that he was in limbo between shoulder pads and a second lieutenant's bars. He had made $5,500 his rookie year with the Eagles, and he and his wife, Barbara, had managed to save $1,200 of it even while driving a new Mercury and living in a hotel apartment best remembered for its Murphy bed. Twelve hundred dollars was going to last only so long, though, so Brookshier surveyed the job market and, years before Bo Jackson and Deion Sanders were born, decided to moonlight in baseball. It was, after all, the sport that had gotten him a scholarship at Colorado. It was also the sport for which some westerners remembered him, either for striking out Kansas catcher Dean Smith, now better known as North Carolina's basketball coach, or for hitting three Missouri batters in a row. "Actually, three batters was nothing," Brookshier says. "One time I almost drilled my own coach – and he was sitting in the dugout."

No problem. In the outback of professional baseball, wild pitchers have historically been as common as cold showers and cheeseburger dinners. At first Brookshier thought he would play for the Lubbock Hubbers of the West Texas–New Mexico League, but the $500 bonus he had been promised never materialized. So he put Lubbock in his rearview mirror and headed for Roswell, where he had grown up pumping gas at his father's Mobil station.

Roswell's population back then was 32,000, and a chief source of excitement was seeing how fast you could travel the 96 miles to a town called Vaughn on a road as straight as a string. ("If you didn't make it in 55 minutes, you were chickenshit," Brookshier says.) It figures, therefore, that a certain amount of fanfare would surround his return from Philadelphia and football's big time to pitch for the Rockets for $225 a week. Sure enough, on April 23, 1954, the *Roswell Daily Record* broke the news by running a picture of his handsome mug and putting his name in headline type almost as big as what Joe Bauman got for hitting two homers against Carlsbad. Unfortunately, it was spelled *Brookshire*.

But nobody on the team ever heard him complain about it. The 72-year-old Bauman, who still lives in Roswell as a retired beer distributor, will testify to that. "Tommy never put himself above us," he says. "He just fell in like an old shoe." Part of the reason for that, no doubt, was Brookshier's respect for Bauman and the Rockets' other bush league icon, Stubby Greer, a third baseman who would finish the season batting .398 to Big Joe's even .400. But the possibility also exists that, in the Longhorn League, Brookshier found the perfect match for his sense of the ridiculous.

First of all, there were the Cubans who populated the Rockets' roster, all of them signed for peanuts by the Washington Senators and shipped to Roswell for seasoning. To say they were raw would be an understatement. "One guy peed in our box of Dixie cups," Brookshier says. But the cup filler was a base-stealing dervish, so he was forgiven his unfortunate choice of urinals. Besides, he gave his teammates one more story to tell on their endless bus trips. "The worst jump we had was down to San Angelo, pretty deep in Texas,"

Bauman says. "We'd leave Roswell at 11:30 or 12 o'clock at night and we wouldn't get down there till past daylight."

Bauman had been kicking around the bushes since 1941. The hole in his big swing kept him from rising any higher than the Eastern League, and now he was two seasons away from ending a career that never paid him more than $4,000 a year. At 22, Brookshier was 10 years Bauman's junior and mesmerized by the netherworld that still has a hold on him. "Every town we played in," he says, "there'd be signs up and down Main Street saying CLOSED – BASEBALL TO-NITE." In those final days before TV started keeping them at home, the Roswell faithful stuffed money through the wire-mesh backstop every time Bauman hit a home run. "He must have doubled his salary," Brookshier says. The ranchers in Midland provided games with a touch of class by wearing shirts as well as pants. "When we'd go to Odessa, there was nothing but tough goddamn wildcatters," Brookshier says, "and they just wore pants and big arms." No matter what the town, though, there always seemed to be an Ace of Clubs bar where ballplayers could drink Lone Star beer and listen to Lefty Frizzell and Ernest Tubb on a bubbling Wurlitzer jukebox. And, yes, there were ladies of the night, too.

"They had a room across the hall from us in Big Spring," Brookshier says. "All night long, we'd hear guys knocking on the door and high heels going across the floor, *click-click-click*. Hell, there wasn't any air conditioning in the place, so it would have been hard enough to sleep anyway. But we'd hear *knock-knock-knock, click-click-click*, too, and then there was always some guy who'd bitch about the price. He'd say, 'Twenty five dollars?' like he was being robbed, and we'd yell, 'Just pay her!'"

Brookshier's partner in that chorus was Bauman, his roommate and, truth be told, a far greater hazard to a good night's sleep than any hooker and her trick. "If I told you Joe snored, you wouldn't get the idea," he says. "What he did was, he tore the damn wallpaper off." Still, Brookshier considered himself lucky, for a Rocket pitcher could have no greater friend that this 6-foot-5 first baseman who ended the season with an astronomical 204 runs batted in. "My philosophy was just hold 'em for Joe," he says.

It worked when he started against Artesia and hung around long enough for Bauman's fifth-inning homer to give him a win. It worked when he came out of the bullpen against Odessa and Bauman dropped that bomb on the rodeo. It even worked when he tried to take matters into his own hands and hit a home run against Big Spring. "The only game I lost was a two-hitter," he says. But the sting of that defeat was eased by the seven victories he piled up even though the steaming fastball of his college days was just a memory. "Pretty soon," he says, "people were calculating that, jeez, if Tommy keeps going like this, he could win 35 games." And then the goddamn Air Force remembered who he was.

One day Brookshier was waiting for Roswell manager Pat Stasey to point him to the pitcher's mound, the next he and his wife were throwing everything they owned into their car and speeding toward Colorado and the Air Force Academy. Not until years later did they realize that they forgot to take any mementos of Brookshier's days as a Rocket. He has no photographs, no newspaper clippings, not even a sweat-stained cap.

Outside of Roswell, where the population has swelled to 45,000, the only tangible proof of what Brookshier did there 40 years ago comes from a curious little book called *Minor League Baseball Stars – Volume III*. In a section devoted to unlikely bushers, he can be found between Sweetwater Clifton, the old Harlem Globetrotter, and New York Governor Mario Cuomo. You see his 7–1 record and his 57 walks in 65 innings, a statistic truly worthy of someone who feels a spiritual connection to Wild Thing Williams. But what really catches your eye is that fat 4.55 earned-run average. "I told you," Brookshier says. "I just tried to hold 'em for Joe."

Philadelphia Magazine, September 1994

7

Hit and Run
The Human Factor

The grace notes go unnoticed. It's the way of baseball, a game where machismo bristles like an unshaven chin. Yet small acts of kindness, wistfulness, even love – eight here if you're keeping score – take place daily within its province. Some I can document, as with the reverence that Tim McCarver showed for playing the game he now threatens to talk to death on TV. Others I imagined, as with my Christmastime reverie about Joe DiMaggio and Marilyn Monroe. And then there was Babe Ruth's house, where I turned for refuge during the 1981 players' strike. It is good to be reminded that the great ones didn't descend from Mount Olympus.

Beginner's Luck

The party came as naturally for the New York Giants as the pennant had – a great whoosh of relief punctuated by the pop of champagne corks and the yells of newly crowned champions bent on getting drunk fast.

It was hard to believe that these same men had just been out in old Ebbets Field grimly going about the business of beating the Brooklyn Dodgers and wrapping up the National League for 1954. But the gears shifted the instant the Giants hit the clubhouse, and no one was more taken by the change than Joey Amalfitano, the bonus boy with a permanent seat on the bench. "The way they acted," he says, "I thought this happened every year." So he stayed in front of his locker, soaking up the celebration, confident he could file away what he saw for future reference.

"Hey, kid."

Larry Jansen had drifted up to Amalfitano's side ready to offer the perspective that came with having just one more big league season left in his pitching arm.

"You better enjoy this now," Jansen said, "because you never know if it'll happen again."

Twenty-seven seasons later, Amalfitano finds himself the unwilling proof of the old pro's pessimism. He played the infield in San Francisco, Houston, and Chicago, and he coached in Chicago, San Francisco, and San Diego, and yet, after all those summers of honorable service, he is farther than ever from the cheers and champagne. He is the manager of the last-place Cubs, the unhappy recipient of a team Preston Gomez couldn't handle, a team destined for the worst record in the league. And sometimes it is all Amalfitano can do to keep from closing his eyes and putting his mind in reverse.

He was an innocent of 20 when New York signed him in '54, a fisherman's son who didn't realize that his $35,000 bonus required the Giants to keep him in the majors for his first two professional seasons, taking up space that should have gone to a veteran capable of contributing. That was the way big league owners kept a check on their spending habits in those days, and there was no arguing with it unless you were a manager. "I never realized until later," Amalfitano says, "how much Leo must have hated to see me sitting on the end of the bench when he was looking for a pinch hitter."

Leo, of course, was the dread Durocher – vain, arrogant, foul mouthed, and an inveterate winner. For each of the two seasons Amalfitano spent with the Giants in New York, Durocher never called him anything except "Kid" and "Hey you." Considering the way their first meeting went, though, it could have been worse. Much worse.

"I was supposed to get together with him at 11:30 a.m. in the lobby of the Adams Hotel in Phoenix," Amalfitano says. "This was a Sunday in February right after I'd signed, and I guess he wanted to get a look at me. Well, 11:30 comes and Leo's not there. It's a quarter to 12 and he still hasn't shown, and I'm getting nervous. I hadn't gone to church yet, and last mass was at 12 o'clock. What could I do? I went to mass.

"When I got back to the hotel, Leo dragged me into the elevator, me and Horace Stoneham, the owner of the club. I was wedged in between the two of them, and Leo was coming down very heavy on me. I'd never been so scared in my life. Finally, he stops to breathe, and I get a chance to tell him I couldn't miss mass. Mr. Stoneham hears that and he steps in between us and says, 'Leo, that's enough.' I'll tell you, I nestled up to Mr. Stoneham real quick."

This was a different world that Joey Amalfitano of the San Pedro, California, Amalfitanos was stepping into. He was a kid who used to take the streetcar to watch Pacific Coast League games in downtown Los Angeles, a sweet dream believer who thought the team from

American Legion Post 65 might be the best one he would ever play on. And suddenly he was transported to the Giants' clubhouse the Sunday before spring training began, with no one else around.

"I sat my bags down," he says, "and I went around the room looking at the names on all the lockers – Mays, Dark, Antonelli. Man, those were names I'd seen in box scores and in the sporting magazines. I was in awe."

Amalfitano would stay that way whether Durocher was rifling pre-game ground balls off his shins or the gentlemanly Alvin Dark was taking him out for dinner and baseball talk. "I knew I wasn't going to play," he says, "so I just did what I was told and tried to stay out of the way." He lockered between Sal Maglie and Monte Irvin, followed the counsel of Maglie and Johnny Antonelli, and pitched early batting practice to Dusty Rhodes and Bobby Hofman, the Giants' artful pinch hitters. "I could throw Dusty 20 straight strikes," he says, "and if my 21st pitch was a ball, he'd be screaming and yelling at me."

But Rhodes's eruptions sounded like a symphony compared to the noises Durocher emitted when he boiled over. Amalfitano heard them for the first time when the Giants fell into last place in Pittsburgh on a May afternoon. "Leo called a meeting and went after the big guys," Amalfitano says. "From then on, we played like hell." And Leo kept raising it, whether he was chewing out a bench-warming slacker or predicting that Rhodes would hit a game-winning, two-strike single off the Dodgers' Billy Loes.

Amalfitano would hear and see it all, a shy kid who got in only nine games, and when it was over, he would have a World Series ring and the pleasure of having seen Willie Mays's fabled catch against Cleveland. A funny guy, that Mays. He drove Amalfitano to and from whatever New York ballpark they happened to be playing in, which was a blessing until the night the Giants clinched the pennant and the party began. "Willie didn't drink," Amalfitano says, "so as soon as he was finished with his interviews, he wanted to get out of there."

The kid followed obediently, but now, as he considers the gray in his sideburns and his Cubs in last place, he realizes he should have stayed a little longer. The memory would have been worth the cab fare.

Chicago Sun-Times, September 5, 1980

AUTHOR'S NOTE: Joey Amalfitano finally made it back to the World Series in 1988 as a coach for the Dodgers. And he got another championship ring, too.

The Buddy System

Ken Brett and Steve Stone shared the rarest of big league phenomena – friendship. The bond between them was formed in sweat, nurtured by mutual honesty, and toasted with the best wine they could find. Then the White Sox traded Brett to California, and he and Stone told each other it was for the best. But they both knew something special was going out of their lives.

Perhaps they should just be glad they were able to be friends for the four months they were together on the Sox pitching staff. They could just as easily have been mere teammates, which seems to be all most ballplayers will let themselves be.

"Professional baseball is a very macho game," Stone says. "Everybody expects you to crush beer cans in your hand and love watching football on TV while you sit around the living room in your underwear. You run the risk of a terrible ribbing if you let your sensitivity show."

To be sensitive enough to establish a genuine friendship is a sure way for players to be labeled "queer" by clubhouse jokers. It takes a certain kind of bravery to ignore such twisted humor. Ask any heterosexual male, athlete or not, who has never expressed his feelings for another man because he was afraid of what people might think.

Brett and Stone were protected somewhat by their sizable reputations among the ladies of the American and National Leagues. Indeed, before Brett left the Sox, he bequeathed to Stone the telephone numbers of his favorite Twentieth Century foxes.

"That was funny," Stone says. "The first time I met him was last winter at one of my restaurants here [in Chicago]. I was standing at the door when he came in and gave his name to the hostess. I went over and introduced myself, but I was really interested in the nice-looking girl he was with."

Stone was a lot more serious in spring training. He was coming back for his second fling with the Sox as a free agent with arm trouble. A potentially severe shoulder injury had limited him to 75 innings as a Cub in 1976, and now, with his 30th birthday creeping up on him, he wondered if he was still good enough to be a big-league pitcher.

"I had worked hard in my career, but not all that hard," he says. "I had never really pushed myself because my talent was always enough to get me by. This time I was in a different situation, and I found out that Kemer (Brett's nickname) was the hardest-working guy on the ball club. So it became a competition kind of thing to see who could work the hardest."

Brett, the left-hander who was the Sox' best pitcher last season, and the right-handed Stone soon discovered they had more in common than a capacity for physical exertion. For one thing, they are among the few major leaguers who use books as something other than paperweights. They had both read the works of Kurt Vonnegut Jr., Richard Brautigan, and Tom Robbins, and Stone made it his duty to see that Brett got turned on to Robert Ludlum's fantasized history. "We had wine in common, too," Stone says. "If you sat both of us down, we could probably drink a couple restaurants dry." They sought out the best places to eat, and over a second or third bottle of choice wine, they began leveling with each other the way few ballplayers do.

"You show bits and pieces of yourself," Stone says, "and pretty soon your true feelings come out. You always need somebody to talk to. It doesn't matter whether you're going good or bad. And you don't just talk about throwing the curveball or how you pitch to Dick Allen. You talk about how you feel the day after you've really gotten pounded, and you help each other deal with depressing situations."

Both men faced crises of confidence this spring. "A lot of pitchers think you're not supposed to admit that," Stone says, "but that's nonsense." So Brett talked about the discomfort of winning with a bloated earned run average, and Stone talked about the misery of pitching well and losing because the Sox weren't scoring any runs for him. "I think I helped Kemer," Stone says. "I know he helped me."

For all their problems, the two of them still found time to laugh. When Stone would pay for $3.50 worth of drinks with a $20 bill, Brett would tell the waitress to keep the change, forcing Stone to explain that his friend was joking. And when they found an unsuspecting audience in the elevator of the building where they each had an apartment, bachelor Brett would start begging Stone to give his wife back and bachelor Stone would leer and say, "But she's so nice."

It took Stone a while Thursday before he learned the laughs were over. The Brett deal sheared the 3 a.m. trading deadline so closely that the morning papers in Boston, where the White Sox were playing, didn't carry the news. A friend had to call Stone and tell him.

At first he was angry. Then he became professionally philosophical, reasoning that the Sox couldn't have signed Brett anyway so they had to get something for him while they could. In the end, though, Stone was simply sad. "I've lost a friend," he said.

Brett flew back to Chicago with the Sox, and he and Stone took their last cab home together. "Kemer was eager to catch up with the Angels," Stone says. "He knows they're going to give him the kind of money he wants. I made him promise that when he gets it, he'll take me out to dinner."

And drink a toast to *auld lang syne*.

Chicago Daily News, June 17, 1977

AUTHOR'S NOTE: As soon as I read Ken Brett's obituary, in November 2003, I knew I would include this piece.

The Big Man Steps Up

When the kids want extra batting practice, Frank Howard throws it. Five hours before duty is supposed to call, with New York's Shea Stadium empty and the sky above it crowded with jet traffic, he works up the kind of lather you don't expect to see even on a manager of the interim variety. He does the work of a humbler servant, insisting that "nothing in baseball is beneath me." He cranks up his right arm for the sake of Darryl Strawberry, Jose Oquendo, and the rest of the Mets' future, but you can't help thinking of Frank Howard's past.

Twenty-five years ago, he was the Dodgers' green giant, a reformed 6-foot-7 basketball player from Ohio State whose feet got tangled as often as his tongue got tied. There were no guarantees that he would make it to the big show, much less render the fences there useless with 382 home runs, but there always seemed to be some tough old bird waiting to cultivate his raw gifts.

In Green Bay it was Pete Reiser, who would have made the Hall of Fame if unforgiving walls hadn't split his skull once too often. "You could strike out four times and make three errors, and Pete wouldn't so much as give you the evil eye," Howard says. "But if you didn't run the 90 feet to first base, he'd humiliate you." So Howard ran, with his head down, taking humble steps that would have befit a man half his 250 pounds, and when he looked up, he was in Spokane, one jump from the majors. Curveballs created a cavern waiting to swallow him, though, and he couldn't cross the cavern until a manager named Bobby Bragan called early muster for him. "I was hitting a buck-50 when he started throwing BP to me," Howard says, "and a month later I was up to .320."

The story takes you to the root of the good works he is attempting now. It connects those private moments with the young Mets and the diligent teacher behind the Louisville Slugger–sized cigar. All Howard asks is that you avoid making too much of his dedication. "That's not just me," he says. "It's baseball's way."

Call it tradition. Victories come hard for the last-place Mets, who are too often the victims of callow youth, insufficient talent, and sagging spirit, but Howard tries to lead them through their rocky times the way he was led through his. He loves the game as he does nothing else, and the air around him is filled with hosannas that he remains part of it.

"What greater honor is there than to be a hitter stepping up against Tom Seaver or Steve Carlton?" he says. "Aw, you might not be so crazy about it at the time, but some day you can tell your kids or your grandkids, 'I did a number on him' or 'He did a number on me.'

"Sure, sometimes the kids on this club think I don't know what the hell I'm talking about. I tell 'em, 'The hell I don't. I carried that lumber back to the dugout damn near 1,500 times, and here I am, still part of baseball.' They don't get any BS from me. They might not hear what they want to hear, but I'm damned if I'll be a f——ing liar. I could look at myself in the mirror every day I played, and I want to do it every day I manage. I don't want to have to apologize to anybody."

Integrity has seldom had such an imposing champion. In his time Frank Howard has been traded and released, hired and fired, and yet he refuses to take his foot off the accelerator. "All I know is that you tee the son of a bitch up and go after it as hard as you can," he says. That was the way he operated when he was fighting for time in the world champion Dodgers' outfield with Duke Snider, Wally Moon, Tommy Davis, and Willie Davis. And when he was the siege gun of the woebegone Washington Senators, flogging as many as 48 homers in a season and driving home as many as 126 runs, Howard still played as if there were a bulldog nipping as his hindquarters.

He overflowed with passion that wouldn't dry up when he became a coach for the Milwaukee Brewers, counseling Gorman Thomas over after-midnight beers, or the manager of the 1981 San Diego Padres, a team that could have killed the spirit of a saint. "Those guys busted their fannies for me," Howard says protectively. "Hell, I just told them, 'I've been run out of 1,000 towns, and I'll be run out of 1,000 more.'"

Maybe that type of thinking made him the perfect man for the Mets. When their sloth and indifference drove amiable old George Bamberger to a hasty retirement two months ago, general manager Frank Cashen needed to find a replacement who wasn't afraid to stick his head in the lion's mouth. The search went no farther than the third-base coach's box, where Howard dwelled. "The people upstairs told me I'd have a temporary arrangement," he says, "and I said, 'Hell, what isn't temporary?'" He was ready to tee it up again.

He should have realized that, sooner or later, he would also get teed off, but Howard is too much the optimist for that. He suggests that the difference between the Mets and a contender is three quality players, and he would have you believe that 99 of every 100 big leaguers understand the virtue of honest toil. There was, however, a post-game meeting with the press in which his displeasure with the Mets carried through the walls of his office, scorching the ears of sinners and melting his image as terminally easygoing.

"Aw, I don't want to always be ragging them," he says. "I've booted balls. I've struck out with a man on third. I know how f——ing tough this game can be. If everything goes up in smoke, I'm not going to put the goddamn blame on anybody. You've got to be a goddamn halfway civilized human being and take responsibility yourself."

That isn't necessarily baseball's way, of course.

But it is Frank Howard's.

Chicago Sun-Times, August 7, 1983

A Little House That Built Ruth

It is one of those Baltimore streets where scrawny dogs run in packs and no bottle lies unbroken. Poverty sticks its tongue out at the progress one block north, and the old men who kill time with wine chuckle mirthlessly at such effrontery. They fear no wrecker's ball, no deluge of fresh brick and mortar, for they have the best insurance policy of all. They have the house where Babe Ruth was born.

Graced by a plaque that says the big day was February 6, 1895, and gussied up with a fresh coat of blue-gray paint, 216 Emory Street stands as more than a life preserver for the poor souls kindness forgot. It is a monument to the slugger who was so much larger than his legend that all the outrageous stories about him turned out to be true. Yes, he loved booze and broads; he loved them just about as much as he did little kids on their deathbeds and bums with their hands out. And the saga of George Herman Ruth started right here, in the second-floor bedroom of a place so small that you can almost touch the front wall with one hand and the back wall with the other.

They charge a buck to walk beneath the rafters that the Babe once shook with cries from his cradle. The price isn't much, but then visitors aren't getting the whole story, for nowhere is there a mention that his mother hustled him out to her parents' home as quickly as she could. Maybe the oversight is on purpose, an unhappy necessity in maintaining the image of the Babe Ruth Birthplace Shrine and Museum. Or maybe, after seven years of business, there are simply too many other things to worry about.

The light in the men's room is burned out and the soda machine is broken. Taped to the front of the cash register is a page of advice from the Baltimore City Police Department about what to do if you are robbed. It's the kind of touch that makes you wonder if there is a reason why, on one of those beautiful summer mornings that proves God's existence, you are the only customer in the joint. "Don't act so surprised," says the woman at the reception desk. "We only had one visitor yesterday, too."

The news seems sacrilegious. You came to the house where Ruth was born expecting to light candles, figuratively if not literally. Always there was the assumption that kindred spirits would be tiptoeing around with you, sizing up the Louisville Slugger the Babe swung for the Yankees and smiling crookedly at the hymnal he was supposed to have used at St. Mary's Industrial School. With big league baseball rendered dormant by the players' strike, what could be more fitting than paying homage to the man whose power and personality saved the game from the taint of the Black Sox scandal? The answer seemed obvious until you set foot in the Ruth family's homestead, and then it got knocked into a cocked hat by statistics. One is the loneliest number.

It makes you wonder if the demolition crew that descended on the Babe's birthplace 14 years ago shouldn't have been allowed to complete its mission. The good burghers of Baltimore weren't without a sense of history, though. They could let New York call Yankee Stadium "the House That Ruth Built," but they wanted something, *anything*, to make sure the world knew whose native son he was.

Two-sixteen Emory Street was it, and 214 and 218 as well. Once an abandoned truck was dragged away from the front door and a mountain of debris was cleared out of the living room, the politicians and businessmen in charge of salvation could see that one address wouldn't be big enough to hold all of the Babe's memorabilia. His birthplace was a Baltimore row house just 12 feet wide and 60 feet long, separated from the neighbors by a thin wall and tied to local lore by a marble stoop of the kind that women still get down on their knees to scrub. But not until three homes had become one could Ruth have his shrine, and even then there were questions about its staying power.

While more important than sentiment in getting the place opened to the public, money was hardly in great supply. The Babe's benefactors turned to Bowie Kuhn for help in raising funds and heard a flunky in the baseball commissioner's office reply: "Babe Ruth Day is out. If we had a Babe Ruth Day, the next thing you know, we'd have a Ty Cobb Day and a Willie Mays Day, and who knows where it would end." So the load had to be carried by Baltimore's business community and a lot of people who never saw the Babe swing a bat in anything except an old newsreel.

For $100 or more, they could sponsor one of Ruth's 714 home runs and be immortalized on a plaque along with the date of the blast and the name of the pitcher Babe hit it off. Hokey as it sounds, the proposition possessed enough charm to still be alive after loosening 500 purse strings around the country. The Babe's widow bought a homer, naturally. So did Brooks Robinson, a graduating high school class in Connecticut, and a mother whose son was 21 when he died in Vietnam.

In one sense, the donors helped clean up bookkeeping; they erased the Ruth house's debt and made it possible for the city of Baltimore to begin operating the shrine. But in another, more important sense, they demonstrated how a saloonkeeper's son and the game he played became part of the fabric of this country. You can feel it when you walk into Babe's birthplace and see the yellowed photographs of him launching another ball toward the great beyond.

It doesn't matter that nobody else is there to have the same chill run up his spine. It might even be better this way. You laugh at the sight of the Babe's silk smoking jacket, the one with "Imperial Hotel" stitched across the back, and you wince at a picture of two men reaching across the vast expanse of his stomach to shake hands. Babe Ruth belonged to each and every one of us as no other athlete ever has. Thirty-three years after his death, with the strike choking the life out of your summer, you realize that more than ever. No wonder you can't wait to see the film clip of the Babe that's supposed to be the highlight of the tour.

"Sorry," says the woman at the cash register. "The fill-um won't be in until Tuesday." There is no hiding the dismay on your face. "If you want, we'll give you a free pass to tour the submarine down in the harbor," the woman says hopefully. Her offer is the perfect metaphor for the season.

Chicago Sun-Times, July 10, 1981

Marilyn and Joe

He stopped sending flowers last fall. I really can't tell you why. For 21 years there had been six red roses delivered three times a week to her pink crypt in Hollywood, and then, in September, there were no more. I suppose you could say the torch that Joe DiMaggio carried for Marilyn Monroe finally went out, but I can't bring myself to do that now. It's the wrong season. It's Christmas.

An odd time to be preoccupied with a stormy romance perhaps, a time that saner and more civilized people may use to think about Mary and Joseph, but I heard a song last week and I can't get it out of my head. It was about Marilyn and Joe dancing in a place where only lovers go, and ever since then I have wondered if they ever spent Christmas together – trimmed a tree, stuffed stockings, sang carols in church, plowed through ribbons and bows, or just held hands by the fire.

Maybe they enjoyed those simple pleasures before they married in January 1954. Maybe DiMaggio, the magnetic Yankee Clipper, somehow convinced the sex symbol who would become his bride that they owed it to themselves to deck the halls with boughs of holly. Maybe Monroe, who divorced him after just nine months, went to her grave thinking that at least there had never been a Christmas like that one.

I can't tell you for sure, though. I can only tell you the way I hope it was. For theirs is a love story that has never died, a surrender of the heart that seemed to grow stronger once they were no longer man and wife, and I am mesmerized by the sweet innocence that has grown up around them.

So don't dredge up the barbiturates with which Monroe took her life. And you might as well forget about throwing in the story of the private eye DiMaggio and Frank Sinatra hired to find out if she was fooling around. I know it's not a perfect world even if you are a center fielder who has been showered with cheers in Yankee Stadium. Nor is everything made copasetic because you are an actress who is suddenly appreciated for your budding comedic genius instead of the curves that got you in the movies in the first place. But I look at what we have now – the knaves and varlets who give us no chance to dream – and I am glad that Monroe and DiMaggio remain in Christmas wrapping paper that never gets thrown away.

She was everything that every other blond bombshell has ever wanted to be, a sexpot who managed to arouse feelings other than sheer animal lust, a heartthrob who received 5,000 letters a week, a heartbreaker who drove one Turkish swain to slash his wrists, a naughty little girl who warded off questions about posing in the nude by saying, "Oh, but I had the radio on."

And he was a Yankee so magnificent that the eminent semanticist Casey Stengel, after seeing him at an old-timers' game, rendered statistics unnecessary by offering this unsolicited endorsement: "We had Mr. DiMaggio that walked out there today and when I tell you that DiMaggio with the cheers he received one of 'em shoulda been given by myself and I shoulda yelled all winter during my off-season because of the success that the club had with him at the bat and the wonderful ketches that he made in the outfield. . . ."

They don't make them like that anymore.

Not like DiMaggio.

Or Monroe.

And we are poorer for it. All we seem to have for heroes are big leaguers trying to burn off their noses with cocaine and old Heisman Trophy winners getting packed off to prison for counterfeiting. There isn't even anyone out there with the gumption of the late Reggie Harding, the 7-footer who failed in the NBA with his hometown Detroit Pistons and then tried to rob a neighborhood grocer who recognized him immediately. "It ain't me," Reggie wailed in protest.

At least he gave us a laugh. Who among today's outlaws can have the same said of them? They aren't terribly amusing, and they aren't terribly romantic, either. Just think of the mean-spirited end to which Steve and Cyndy Garvey came. Or the smarmy double entendres that Jimmy Connors and Chris Evert trade now that each is married to someone else. Or the rumors of an ex-NFL running back's messy dalliance with one of Hollywood's heavenly bodies. No wonder I seek refuge in what Monroe and DiMaggio gave us.

Somehow divorce made their love more poignant, more fetching. There was no pitcher who ever made DiMaggio suffer the way he did when he was apart from Monroe, and his suffering almost brought her back to him, or so it is said. There were rumors that they would marry again and live in San Francisco and try to keep their planets from colliding. Then she died by her own hand, and DiMaggio donned the mourning clothes he hasn't removed since.

He let only 23 people into her funeral, none of them from Hollywood. He kissed her on the forehead and whispered, "I love you, I love you," before her carved bronze casket was sealed. And he started sending the roses that didn't stop coming until 21 years later.

None of us may ever know why, because Joe DiMaggio isn't a man of explanations. But he has shown us his heart anyway, shown it more openly that any of society's romantic exhibitionists would have. With quiet dignity and elegant grace, he has left no doubts that there hasn't been a Christmas since her death that he hasn't wanted to share with Marilyn Monroe. On this day, on any day, we should all be loved so well.

Chicago Sun-Times, December 25, 1983

The Clown

Before he could shout tall orders to the St. Louis Browns' pinch-hitting midget and bellyache about being shortchanged by George Steinbrenner, before he could get squeezed out of an All-Star game by Richard Nixon and make Satchel Paige his comedy partner, before he could knock 'em dead at the Smithsonian and wonder if anyone would ever let him into the Hall of Fame, Max Patkin had to endure the misfortune of throwing a fastball where Joe DiMaggio could knock it lopsided.

Though DiMag was quick to make the most of the pitch's location, there was no way he could have failed to notice that Max looked like something the cat dragged in. This was in 1944, and he was even skinnier than he is now, a 6-foot-3 coat hanger with a neck that could have served as a fire hose, ears the size of barn doors, and a nose that weighed as much as a newborn babe. Bill Veeck, the Barnum of baseball, would eventually decide that Max was put together by someone who had trouble reading instructions. But first there was the matter of DiMaggio and an army-navy game in Hawaii that needed comic relief, which was, of course, the only kind of relief Max could provide.

"We were losing 7–0 in the first inning when I came in," he says, "and the first time I faced DiMaggio, I struck him out. Me, a Class D pitcher in the navy, the funny-looking SOB everybody always laughed at. And I loved it. Oh, man, I'm telling ya, I really gave it the big ham when I did that."

The pitch that put a K beside DiMaggio's name in the scorebook was not, however, the one that helped Patkin break the laugh barrier. The pitch that did that was the one Joltin' Joe pounded over the fence and into the wild blue yonder.

"Longest home run I've ever seen," Patkin says. "I stood there admiring it for a while, and then, when Joe rounded first base, I had this inspiration. I started running with him, imitating him. It was an ad-lib. I didn't know what the hell he was going to do. But he just kept running – gliding really, like an antelope – and when we finally got to home plate, his whole team was out waiting for us. They didn't want to shake Joe's hand; they wanted to shake mine. Can you believe it? They loved what I did, and there were 10,000 service guys in the park going crazy, too. Everybody went along with the gag."

Max Patkin had found his calling. He could make people laugh, and making people laugh would keep him in baseball, the only place he had ever dreamed of being since he grew up funny in West Philadelphia. Naturally, he doubted his staying power; he was handed his release from professional baseball, in Wilkes-Barre, Pennsylvania, in 1946. But by the end of that season, he was Veeck's resident clown with the Cleveland Indians. No longer did anybody care about his days as a sore-armed right-hander who once threw a pitch so high and outside that it hit a sportswriter minding his own business in the press box. All the paying customers wanted to see was Max make his head go one way while his body went the other.

He has been at it ever since. Come June 2, in Nashville, he will begin his 40th season of twisting his rubber face into shapes only a Halloween mask maker could appreciate and covering himself with dirt in the first-base coach's box. He has 72 dates booked, and they will take him all the way to Vancouver, a journey he promises to make if he has to carry his own luggage over the mountains. So kindly salute Max by wearing your baseball cap sideways, the way he always does. At age 65, he isn't just another senior citizen. He is the last true comic the playing ranks are likely to produce.

The reason for Max's exalted status should be obvious. He comes from a time when baseball people realized that what he brought to the game was fun, not sacrilege. Consider his debut in Detroit, when Max pretended to give Hank Greenberg, the Tigers' great first baseman, a hotfoot, and Greenberg did more than go along with the gag. He improved on it. "He jumped up and down like I'd really burned him," Max says, "and then he picked me up and shook me like a sack of potatoes. Right there in Tiger Stadium, with the people hanging from the rafters. I'm telling ya, it was great."

But as Astroturf, cookie-cutter stadiums, and the designated hitter encroached on baseball, the funny bone was taken out of it. More and more, he found the majors populated by grumps like Ralph Houk, who was managing the Yankees when Steinbrenner shipped Max in for a few laughs. "Houk came running up to me with his fists clenched, screaming, 'You're not gonna coach!'" Max says. "He told me they were fighting for a pennant. I told him it was April."

No wonder Max has left the big leagues to two worthy comic figures, the Famous Chicken and the Phillie Phanatic, and a host of inferior feathered creatures. He still owns the sky blue blazer with the patch that tells the world who he is: "Max Patkin, Clown Prince of Baseball." And besides, he has always felt more at home in the minors anyway.

Down there, he doesn't get the kind of money Steinbrenner gypped him out of by paying just $600 for two weekends' work – but he won't get his heart broken the way he did when President Nixon's late arrival at the 1970 All-Star Game canceled his greatest shot at fame. Down there, he can remember how it was when Reggie Jackson played in Lewiston, Idaho, and Pete Rose was in Macon, Georgia. It was a time when a Pacific Coast League umpire pulled a blank gun and shot him twice. And when Paul Owens, the Phillies' manager, was a Canadian-American League first baseman who got his signals crossed and missed a throw that rearranged Max's schnozz.

Reminiscing makes Max young again, and that is no small achievement. "I still run good and I still get the laughs; I can still make the faces and I still got the body movement good," he says, "but sometimes I have to stop to catch my breath." This summer, as he feels the lingering effects of back surgery, he may have to stop more often than ever. "I couldn't sleep, I couldn't walk, I couldn't straighten up," he says, "so I had to do something." In another week, he will start exercising, and two weeks after that, he will hit the road again, eager to coach three innings for any home team that will have him.

No million-dollar payoffs are waiting, and the national spotlight will never reach the places he works. But he is fueled by the pride of being the lone survivor of a breed America doesn't recognize anymore, a breed that included Al Schacht, Jackie Moore, and a lot of other names that have been swallowed by time.

If Max needs anything more to keep him going, it is the thought of how the kids in Omaha line up to get his autograph – them with their pencils and scraps of paper, him hot and dirty in his baggy uniform. "You ought to see it," he says. And he looks around the Valley Forge condominium where he lives with the plaques and pictures that hang on one wall. His daughter is sleeping in another room, his brother is at work, his ex-wife has remarried, and he is thinking about the kids in Omaha.

"How many other things I got left in my life?" Max Patkin asks.

Philadelphia Daily News, May 7, 1985

AUTHOR'S NOTE: Max Patkin died in 1999, and I got the impression that his last years weren't easy ones. But he did land a small role in *Bull Durham* that was made bigger by the fact that it called for him to dance with Susan Sarandon. Maybe the clown got the last laugh after all.

Rocky's Road

Baseball executives by and large dislike seeing tobacco juice spattered on their office carpets, although nobody has ever figured out whether this is because they admire good manners or abhor cleaning bills. In either case, 35 years in the game have taught Rocky Bridges to keep his great expectorations to himself when he is indoors. Rocky's unexpected rapprochement with couth has forced his myriad admirers to search for other reasons why he isn't managing a big league team. The explanation that turns up most often, as fate would have it, involves the one other unforgettable thing that comes out of his mouth: the truth.

It was he who once surveyed the Phoenix Giants after they had dragged him into last place and announced, "If this is a ball club, my rear end is a Japanese typewriter." It was he who started a Pacific Coast League season on the road by proclaiming, "I can't spell Albuquerque, but I can smell it." And it was he who declined fisticuffs with a roughneck busher on a midsummer's night by confessing, "I couldn't whip the muscles in that guy's sweat."

For such honorable and creative service, Rocky has been awarded a seventh season in Phoenix, where the seats never get filled and the heat never stops. "We're about three blocks from hell in the summertime," he says. "It's a great farm club if you're sinful." [Author's note: This was before the advent of the Arizona Diamondbacks.] Sinful he isn't, though, unless it's a capital offense to devote a lifetime to developing players like Andy Messersmith and Jack Clark while keeping the paying customers laughing. Rocky's young charges even won a Coast League championship in 1977, but by then he already had taken one all-expenses-paid trip to San Francisco and interviewed for a job he never was going to get.

"The Giants were ready to hire Joe Altobelli, so I think they were just giving me a courtesy call," he says. "It wasn't anything I was gonna go cry about. Sure, I'd like to manage a big league club – I'd be squirrelly if I didn't – but I haven't gone and started no advertising campaign for Rocky Bridges. Hell, it wouldn't be worth the trouble. Seems to me that when you manage in the majors, all you're really doing is walking out on the gangplank and waiting for the guy with the sword to come and poke you in the butt."

The truth in those words is mixed with self-defense as the 53-year-old Bridges faces another Phoenix summer with a last-place team that is already 11 1/2 games out of first place. It is that time of year when the big leagues' unlucky managers start getting it in the neck, but even though every executive in baseball can get his number in an instant, Rocky doesn't expect any calls.

In their absence, he jollies himself with life's small pleasures. He does business in a city where it is safe to walk the three miles from his home to the ballpark, and he has an office jammed with copies of *Home & Garden* magazine and enough chewing tobacco to sink the Titanic all over again. Even so, the Phoenix Giants may have the better of the deal. After all, no other team in baseball gets to play for a manager who shakes his head at the sight of a luckless pitcher and says, "If it was raining nickels, he'd be in jail. If it was raining camel crap, he'd be in the middle of the field without a number."

The kids who play for Rocky are special to him, whether they are laughing or learning. "They're just starting to think they know everything by the time they get to Triple A," he says. "If they thought any more of themselves, they probably wouldn't hustle the way they do." Above all else, Rocky demands hustle, the kind he suspects big leaguers forget, the kind a left fielder named Chris Bourjos gives him daily.

"The kid had to take the bus from Chicago to Cedar Rapids before anybody would sign him," Rocky says. "Hell, you got to love him just for that. And run? He runs out everything like it was a triple. The kid don't know quit."

In that respect, Chris Bourjos is a lot like Rocky Bridges. To hear Rocky tell it, he never had a bad day in baseball, even though he describes his 11-year career in the majors as "nondenominational." He was a stumpy journeyman infielder who bounced from Brooklyn to Cincinnati to Washington to Detroit to the expansion Los Angeles Angels, ringing up a .248 lifetime batting average, earning $12,000 in his best year, and spending off-seasons as a ditch digger and a laborer in a Boraxo factory. "For some reason," he says, "my wife insisted that our four kids had to eat." Rocky didn't complain. Even now, he insists the worst thing that ever happened to him was getting traded away from Cincinnati as soon as he learned to spell it.

He's funny that way. He honestly believes he is in baseball's debt. "It got rid of my real name for me," he says. "Hell, I got four Labrador retrievers I wouldn't name Everett Lamar Bridges." Beyond that, baseball let him smoke big league cigars, gave him a seat on the Dodgers' bench during a World Series, and even found a spot for him on the 1958 American League All-Star team. "Mantle, Williams, all those guys was in the dressing room," he says. "I didn't go around getting autographs, but I felt like it."

Rocky lasted three more seasons as a player, and then he became what he is now – a teacher. He has coached with the Angels in the majors and managed in the minors at San Jose, Hawaii, and Phoenix, and every step of the way, he has delivered the same message: "You got to make the big show, kid. It's the only letterman's sweater to have." In an era short on inspiration, his pitch has worked with everybody except the people who hire major league managers. A lesser man would wonder about himself, maybe even consider spending the winter in Arizona and the summer in Idaho instead of the other way around, but Rocky insists there are no rocks in his head.

"I'm still smart," he says. "It's those other guys I'm worried about."

Chicago Sun-Times, June 2, 1980

Last Licks

Everything about the kid smacked of a storybook rookie who had checked his straw hat and cardboard suitcase at the clubhouse door and still couldn't shake the hayseed from his crew-cut hair. It was 1959, so the crew cut was all right, but when the St. Louis Cardinals got a load of the rest of him – the brown shoes and the red Banlon shirt and the plaid sport coat – they knew an innocent was in their midst.

They called him "Bush," which was short for bush leaguer. The kid didn't mind. He was 17 years old, still eligible for American Legion ball back home in Memphis, and here he found himself in the company of Stan Musial, Bob Gibson, and Ken Boyer – all the names he had heard Harry Caray spout on the radio. To say the kid felt out of place is to belabor the obvious. But *why* he felt out of place . . . ah, that is a fire engine of a different color.

The truth of the matter was that he had yet to fall in love with the Cards. True, they had signed him for a $75,000 bonus, and, true, he was their catcher of the future – two facts that would seem to dictate immediate allegiance. But when he showed up in Milwaukee, fresh out of the minors and primed for his first day in the big show, he couldn't forget that he had spent his childhood cheering for Henry Aaron and the Braves. So as Aaron came to bat, the kid leaned forward in the St. Louis dugout and yelled, "Come on, Henry!"

"The veterans," Tim McCarver says, "gave me the dirtiest looks I'd ever seen."

What those Cards couldn't have suspected was that 21 years later, McCarver would still be savoring their scorn as he took his place in baseball history. When he put on his Philadelphia Phillies uniform this season, he became just the eighth big leaguer to play in four decades. By the deceptively simple act of stepping between the white lines, he joined ranks with Ted Williams, Mickey Vernon, Early Wynn, Bobo Newsom, Minnie Minoso, Jim Kaat, and Willie McCovey. At the same time, however, McCarver also managed to establish himself as unique. "I'm the first catcher who's ever done it," he says. But lest anyone accuse him of pomposity, he is prepared to let the air out of his own balloon. "I'd like to think I'm more than a novelty," he says, "but you don't have to look too hard to realize that this is an accommodation."

Originally, McCarver wanted to play the entire season, calling pitches for old friend Steve Carlton every fourth day and standing ready to pinch-hit the rest of the time. The Phillies' brain trust had other plans. "They called me in at the end of last year and said, 'You could really help this club next season,'" McCarver recalls. "I said, 'Really?' and they said, 'Yeah. Quit.'"

McCarver went quietly, buoyed by the promise that he would be back when the roster expanded this September 1 and reassured by the thought that he wouldn't be far from the Phillies even out of uniform. He was going to do color commentary on their radio and TV broadcasts, an assignment guaranteed to keep him within range of the clubhouse bull sessions he could never get enough of. "I would have really been lost if I'd been stuck in an office job in Great Falls, Montana," he says. Moreover, the Phillies might not have paid his airfare back to Philadelphia. As it was, all he had to do was descend from the press box and remember his way to the plate.

"Once I checked an old press guide and saw that I hit left-handed, I was fine," McCarver says. At the very least, he was well enough prepared to walk against Los Angeles on the first day of his return and to fly out to right field against St. Louis 12 days later. "We lost both games big," he says, "so you couldn't say they were counting on me to save them in the clutch."

He can tell you about his first big league hit, an infield single against the Cubs' Glen Hobbie in Wrigley Field, and the three-run homer with which he beat the Yankees in the '64 World Series. He can tell you how it felt to be part of the precision-crafted '67 Cardinals and to have the folks in Memphis name the local minor league park after him. If McCarver has a message, though, it is one of good times that almost got away.

"It's funny," he says. "When you're living those moments, you don't fully appreciate them. You're just too busy playing the game."

He finally realized his oversight in the mid-'70s, after bouncing from St. Louis to Philadelphia to Montreal, back to St. Louis, then on to Boston and almost out of baseball. "I was waived and released in two years, and I couldn't understand it," he says. "They preach competition and desire and fire and hustle, and then they expect you to take your uniform off very meekly."

McCarver refused to surrender, which was where Steve Carlton came in. Their friendship had been forged in the old days on the Cardinals, and now the strong-willed Carlton was determined to see them reunited in Philadelphia. He would pitch and McCarver would catch and that would be that. To the surprise of many, it was. Before they were finished, McCarver had salted away his best batting average ever – a plump .320 – and Carlton had won his second Cy Young Award. "I'd like to tell you more," McCarver says, "but. . . ."

He has to get in one more swing in batting practice. A voice behind him has warned that he is down to his last seven seconds, the pitcher is midway through his windup, and McCarver is already shouting that these kids don't respect their elders. Shouting and jumping in to take that last swing and generally having a hell of a good time. After all, these are the last best days of his life. No sense in wasting them.

Chicago Sun-Times, September 21, 1980

8

These Bees Are Bad News

"Bad News Bees, huh?" says an early arrival at Municipal Stadium, eyeing the message on a player's T-shirt.

"The bad news," the player informs him, "is we're here."

The catcher travels by skateboard and lives in a ballpark storage room that he decorated by painting a likeness of Charles Manson on the door. The left-hander claims he drove the nearly 400 miles from Los Angeles in 4 1/2 hours, which is roughly the speed at which cocaine chased him out of the big leagues. The third baseman detests day games, or else he wouldn't have had to gobble amphetamines to get up for them when he was a Cub.

And you should have seen the ones who got away.

Leading off was Derrel Thomas, who decided he was due for a promotion after so dutifully serving the Giants, Dodgers, and Phillies as a clubhouse lawyer. Exiled to baseball's bushes, Thomas didn't want to just play center field for the San Jose Bees; he wanted to manage them, too. It was as if he hadn't heard the news about himself.

Go ahead and drag out the way his name came up in last year's double-ugly Pittsburgh drug trial if you must. But the real rap on Thomas concerned the time he once picked to wash his car up the road in San Francisco – during a game. Anyone who appointed him as a leader of men would always have to worry that he might choose the fifth inning to lead them to a hose and a pail of soapy water.

So the answer was no. But Thomas persisted, and when persistence didn't do him any good, he opted for insolence. As the Bees worked on relay plays, he interrupted Harry Steve, the man who had the job he coveted, and announced, "That's not the way the Dodgers did it." Steve responded the only way possible for a manager who is also team president and general manager: he released Thomas. It was not yet opening night.

By the time that momentous occasion arrived, 2 1/2 weeks ago, Mike Norris was at the top of whatever game he was playing. Outwardly, he didn't appear bothered that he was still dodging the ghosts of his dalliance with nose candy instead of starting another 20-victory season as the linchpin of the Oakland A's pitching staff. He was the clubhouse clown who greeted everyone with a singsong "Hey-hey-hey-hey." Nothing seemed to please him more than wandering out to shortstop in his street clothes so he could field grounders with a glove on one hand and his other hand in his pocket. But when the Bees really needed Norris, he wasn't there.

Maybe he was preoccupied with what the Internal Revenue Service was trying to do to him. Surely there was enough noise about his lack of a driver's license when he started showing up late for games. "Mike should have been responsible enough to make arrangements for a ride," Harry Steve says. But Mike wasn't. The first time, he got docked a week's pay and the chance to start the Bees' third game. The second time, Steve kept pushing back the deadline, telling the players they would vote on whether Norris should remain with the team. The extended deadline had been history for 10 minutes when Norris finally walked in the door. When he walked back out, it was forever.

"Right now I worry about him in his everyday life," Steve says. "Wherever he's going, he's got a problem, even if it's just being irresponsible."

But there are others among the Bees who know a last chance when they see one, and they are making the most of it. Not only does Steve Howe look like Godzilla against the California League's predominantly fuzzy-cheeked hitters, he has proved an unerring marksman in the same kind of urinalysis that sunk his career with the Dodgers. Daryl Sconiers isn't spilling a drop, either, as he tries to rediscover the sweet swing that had the Angels dreaming he would be the second coming of Rod Carew. And what of Ken Reitz, ex-Cardinal, ex-Giant, ex-Cub, ex-Pirate, pedaling around Muni on a girls' 12-speed bike because the law says he can't drive and praying that 34 isn't too old to make it all the way back from amphetamine addiction?

Can these Bees really be such bad news?

"If that's what we were," Howe says, "we'd paint the team bus black and put 'F—— Me' on the front of it."

The lords of baseball may well be expecting as much, for this is truly the game's legion of the damned. In addition to their three scandal-tainted stars, the Bees employ three other big league wash-outs, half a dozen Japanese players and a bunch of sandlot escapees who aren't supposed to have enough talent to play even Class A ball. The result looms as more than a feast for the California League's grandstand sadists. It is a gamble that could render Harry Steve, and the Bees, past tense.

"If Harry doesn't win this year," Howe says, "he's going to be picking olives in Crete."

§ Steve Howe can't stand still.

He is here to grab a handful of grapes and there to suggest that the Bees include pelvic thrusts in their warm-up exercises. Here to put his cap on sideways and there to tell the Japanese players that they need to know only one word to survive in this country: Budweiser. Here to polish up his statistics (seven hits in 14 1/2 innings) and there to inform the gentleman calling from CBS in Los Angeles, "My goal in life was not to become a professional ballplayer and become addicted to chemicals."

"Kind of hyper, isn't he?" Harry Steve whispers.

Hyper and, at age 28, impatient.

Howe wants baseball commissioner Peter Ueberroth to believe that he is clean, but until recently the commissioner's office wasn't returning his phone calls. "If they're going to treat it as a good-boy, bad-boy situation, I definitely don't fall into the bad-boy category,"

Howe says. His case history with the Dodgers and the Twins suggests otherwise, however, so Ueberroth is letting him dangle before approving any deal that could get him back to the big show.

"Put me against any left-hander in baseball right now, and I'll get a job," Howe says. "All I ask for is a chance to get a job."

But the game was always easy for him. It was the rest of life that threw him a curve. Sometimes, when he stops ricocheting around the ballpark and starts thinking, he realizes it. Compare him with Mike Norris, for instance. The Bees threw Norris the same life preserver they threw Howe, but Norris threw it back.

"It becomes a choice," Howe says. "Sooner or later, you have to take responsibility for your actions."

The life preserver fits him nicely – so far.

§ Hold an old-timers' game in San Jose 10 or 15 years from now and you'll be able to ring up such fancy names as George Brett, Dennis Leonard, and Jay Johnstone. You might even get lumpy, lovable Rocky Bridges to return to the city where he first said, "I managed good but, boy, did they play bad."

The problem is, there might not be a professional team here then. There might not even be one next year. Never mind the covetous glances the city fathers cast at the Giants when they were being shopped around last winter. Never mind the 675,000 people who live within the city limits or the 1.2 million people who live in Santa Clara County. Never mind the high-tech wonders that are worked daily here in the heart of Silicon Valley. This is a dying franchise.

It is not just that the Bees last had a winning season in 1979; it is that they have lost 259 games in the past three years alone. And their attendance shows it. In the league's largest market, they drew 53,423 paying customers last year, and only two of nine teams did worse. What's more, the Bees have no big league affiliation to infuse them with playing talent. The closest they come is an agreement with Japan's Seibu Lions, and the Lions, bless their hearts, are more than an ocean away from such old providers as the Royals, Expos, Mariners, and Angels when it comes to baseball.

Harry Steve knew things weren't going to improve when the Blue Jays turned up their noses at a chance to put a farm team in San Jose and settled instead on Ventura. "The park there doesn't even have lights," Steve says. But he has an idea why it happened: "The last year we had a player development contract, I clashed with someone who's pretty powerful, a farm director. He wouldn't have the guts to tell me to my face what he's been saying, but I've heard about it."

Maybe that makes Steve an outlaw of sorts. If so, he knows how to play the part. There is no modesty when he talks about tracking down Howe at his winter home in Whitefish, Montana. Rather, Steve poses with a cigarette in the corner of his mouth, trying to look older than 30, and says, "It was just a matter of a general manager having enough balls to go after Howe. The A's got Andujar, the Mets got Hernandez. What's the difference?"

The difference is that no one ever thought the A's and the Mets were running halfway houses. With Harry Steve's Bad News Bees, it was just the opposite. He might as well have said, "Give me your poor, your tired, your huddled masses," because every vagabond in baseball started calling. Not just the drug cases, but the outcasts like Darryl Cias, the catcher who bounced from the A's to Italy in one season. And Fernando Arroyo, a pitcher who slipped through Oakland, Detroit, and Minnesota almost unnoticed. And Lorenzo Gray, a third baseman who got pink-slipped by the White Sox after batting nearly .400 in the Pacific Coast League three years ago.

It was a windfall, but an expensive one, considering that some of these characters were going to make upwards of six times the California League's $300 minimum monthly salary. Steve decided the financial risk was worth it on the grounds that you have to spend money to make money. "I've always paid my bills, although sometimes they've been late," he says. "This year, if things don't work out, they're going to be later than usual."

But look at the bright side. If things *do* work out, attendance will be like opening night's 4,911 and not like the season low 488. If nobody on the team goes over the wall, Steve might be able to sell one of his stars to a big league team, a deal that would give both the player and the Bees a share of the money. "You look at Toronto," he says, "and you know they may be only a Steve Howe away from the World Series."

But do the Blue Jays know it? That is one more worry for Harry Steve, who already has more worries than he bargained for. His biggest one, of course, is managing the team. He thought a proven minor league commodity named Frank Verdi was going to do it, but five days before spring training, the Yankees lured Verdi away with a scouting job.

"I didn't want to get another manager just to get another manager," Steve says. "I had handpicked the ball club, and I wanted to hire a guy who would follow through on the plans I had." He smiles slyly. "Plus I'd used all my money signing players."

Thus did Steve add another line to a resume that shows no evidence whatsoever of his ever having played pro ball. Even on the sandlots back home in Youngstown, Ohio, he was never much of an infielder. "Decent glove, crummy arm, even worse hitter," he says. "I always knew what to do, but I couldn't do it." No wonder he became a general manager. He was 23 when he dropped out of Biscayne College's sports administration program to run Macon in the South Atlantic League. Ever since, he has been swimming against the tide in San Jose. And now he is a manager who can't help thinking he really isn't doing things the Dodgers' way, who hasn't mastered the art of hitting fungoes, who can't even get thrown out of a game in high style.

"You're the worst manager in the league," said the umpire who bounced him in Fresno the other night.

Steve considered the possibility. Then he said, "Well, you're the worst umpire in the league."

Obviously, this will take some getting used to.

§ "They tell you you're not supposed to take the game home with you," Darryl Cias says, "but that's tough to do when you live at the ballpark."

His home is the storage room under the first-base grandstand.

He calls it "the Stadium Hilton" even though the do-not-disturb sign hanging on the door was borrowed from a Holiday Inn. The reason he lives there is as easily understood as an empty wallet.

There wasn't much money to be made when Cias played in Italy last season, and the bright future he thought he had catching for the A's went up in smoke the year before that. "I hit .300 my rookie year in Oakland," he says, "and the next spring they wanted to send me to Double A. From what I understand, they thought I had a bad attitude, didn't want to work. Listen, I'd rather have a drug rap than that."

Whatever, Cias needed a cheap place to stay. When Harry Steve told him about the two Bees who had lived in the Hilton last season, the thing Cias liked most was that they lived there free. So in he moved. Ken Reitz followed soon afterward, motivated by the lack of a driver's license, which put him on a short leash. There was a pitcher living with them until he got released, as well as a steady stream of teammates looking for a cold beer and reporters seeking an oddball story. "We threw another mattress on the floor," Cias says, "and the guy from *Rolling Stone* stayed the night with us."

With all the company, Cias decided it wasn't enough to have the place decorated with a couple of makeshift beds and six stadium chairs propped in front of a portable TV. He rooted around in the remnant bin at a carpet store and found enough scraps to cover the concrete floor. He decorated the walls with a poster for a skin flick called *Bubble Gum*. He found a neon Coors sign to use as a night light. His most dramatic contribution, however, was to paint Charles Manson's face on the door.

Cias warmed up for his masterpiece by painting the TraveLodge and Almaden Hyundai signs on the outfield fence. When he started to put a coat of black paint over the Hilton's drab tan walls, Reitz stopped him and held up a paperback copy of the book *Helter Skelter*. "Why don't you paint him?" Reitz asked, pointing at Manson's wild-eyed mug on the cover. Cias obliged, and a conversation piece was born.

But sometimes, early in the morning, he can't help wondering if

Manson's wacko likeness isn't getting to his roommate. "I'll wake up," he says, "and Reitzie will be sitting there, staring at it."

§ If Daryl Sconiers couldn't tell where he was by the lack of soap in the shower, he would be able to by the paucity of clean socks and jocks or the lights that make him feel like he's trapped in perpetual dusk. Even an innocent conversation can serve as a reminder that his next step down will take him out of baseball.

"Where'd you play last year, man?" Sconiers asks the Bakersfield Dodger who has just camped beside him after hitting a single.

"Pioneer League," the kid chirps.

"Damn."

That is what baseball has come to for the 27-year-old Sconiers. When the Angels released him last winter, after a season in which cocaine brought him to his knees, there were no takers. "People tell you you're supposed to be one of the best left-handed hitters, and then something like that happens," he says. "It gave me a feeling that people were just fed up, that teams weren't taking risks."

Sconiers's campaign in San Jose is to convince the world that he is no risk at all. Part of it is based on the kind of talking that sounds like it comes straight from a therapist's couch. He thinks back to his three seasons with the Angels and says, "I suffered from belligerent intolerance. I got used to all those luxuries we had in the majors, people offering to drive your car around front and pick you up after the game. I didn't realize that didn't have anything to do with reality. I was unbearable, selfish, couldn't deal with other people's mistakes. Really. You look up 'belligerent intolerance' in the dictionary and you'll see that was Daryl Sconiers over and over again."

Maybe insight and humility come when you are forced to live the way he is, in a Holiday Inn, with his wife and child back in Southern California and without a moment's relief from the fear that this might be the end. "I think I have time to make it back," he says, "but I don't have time to waste."

It is a precarious situation, and there are nights when Sconiers can't escape it, nights like this one. He strikes out swinging his first time up against Bakersfield, then goes down looking the next time. When the third strike is called, he takes two steps across the plate and slings his bat against the grandstand wall. And then Municipal Stadium closes in on him.

From the third-base seats, a schoolyard taunt: "Throw your bat, Daryl."

From the first-base seats, a regulation-issue insult: "You're a bum!"

Back to the third-base seats for a final, withering judgment: "Weak, weak, weak."

In a ballpark with only 5,000 seats, there is neither the distance nor the dull hum to be found in the big leagues. Every insult is right in Sconiers's ears, and when he talks back, the abuse becomes louder and more cutting. His best defense is the single he pumps into right field in the seventh inning. But even that backfires when he over-runs second base on a bunt and stands helplessly between second and third, waiting to be tagged out, waiting so long that he might have time to compose what he will say the next afternoon: "Years from now, I want people to tell you, 'Daryl Sconiers, he endured.'"

It is a wonderful thought, and yet it sounds all wrong. When you're at a revival, you don't expect to hear an epitaph.

Philadelphia Daily News, April 29, 1986

9

Hit and Run

First Person

Hardly a day passes that I don't think about the joy I took from playing baseball as a kid. I chased after the game long after it had any use for me, and I've never regretted a moment of it. Baseball gave me an identity, a refuge, and, best of all, friendships that have endured over the years. The four essays I offer here are as much for those friends as they are for me.

Beautiful Dreamers

He wore the look of a hard life, his face seamed with wrinkles, his hands thick with calluses. He would pull up to the park in a truck as worn and dirty as his plumber's coveralls, and his first stop was always the men's room behind the wooden grandstand. He traded his work boots for spiked shoes in there and put on a uniform that had TED'S GLASS written across the chest. When he walked back out, he was both a third baseman and a ghost of his own past.

He'd had a chance to be a Yankee – that's what the geezers in the stands said. The Yanks had shipped him to Twin Falls after World War II, and damned if he wasn't leading the Pioneer League in hitting when his temper boiled over once too often. The next thing anybody knew, he was back home, toting a lunch bucket and playing for nothing more than the joy of swinging at scuffed baseballs in the fading twilight. Funny how I remember him all these years later, but I do. It is from the figure he cut and the stories his presence evoked that I trace my fascination with old ballplayers.

I was 14 that summer I discovered him at Municipal Park in Salt Lake City, and a voice in my head told me there were lessons to be learned from him and his kind, that maybe an old ballplayer was even something to be. My family and I had just moved from Los Angeles, and we were renting a house a few blocks from Muni, so I was playing in two kids' leagues during the day and watching the old guys in the evenings. Most of them were barely in their twenties, of course, but the ones I watched closest had more age on them. They hadn't made it in pro ball, or they had never been good enough to get that far in the first place, and still they couldn't give up the game. Even when they had wives and kids and jobs and mortgages to worry about, baseball remained their love, their passion. But if you had put it to them in those words, they would have clocked you the way I saw a mousy center fielder get it when he forgot that the first baseman he was fighting was left-handed.

What they played for in the Salt Lake Amateur League wasn't money. It was for the chance to hit a home run into the towering cottonwood trees in left field. And to knock the sneer off the face of the farmer who had enough heat on his fastball to pitch wearing a watch. And to laugh at the shortstop whose shoulder came out of its socket every time he reached up to catch a pop fly. And to talk about it all afterward while they leaned against their cars, beers in hand, wives gone to make dinners that would surely be cold by the time the old ballplayers got home.

My first tentative steps into their company came when Ted's Glass rewarded me for an hour of shagging balls by letting me pitch the final minutes of batting practice. That was heady stuff for a third baseman just out of the eighth grade, and it might have been as good as it got, for a strong arm was one of my few virtues in baseball. But a year later, a cantankerous former minor leaguer convinced me that catcher was the only position for someone who ran as slowly and loved the game as much as I did. If he hadn't done that, I never would have heard the praise of a Boston Red Sox scout when I was in high school. And I never would have gone to college on a baseball scholarship. And I never would have had a place to land after I walked away from that scholarship as a sophomore because I had fallen under the spell of books. When I was on vacation, Utah Power & Light figured I could still find my way around behind the plate. It wasn't the big leagues – it was the Amateur League – but I had the time of my inconsequential career.

For the next three summers, I played on a team stocked with college studs, erstwhile pros and beautiful dreamers – a team that twice won championships and never stopped laughing. In a closet at home, I even have a trophy that says I was UP&L's most valuable player in 1967, and I blush at how much pride it still gives me.

But valuable though I may have been, nobody ever mistook me for our best player. I hit almost .400 and still ended up 70 points behind a first baseman with a million-dollar swing and a 10-cent knee. Maybe that's why I get just as big a kick out of remembering the pitcher who stuck out his tongue every time he threw a curve. Or the third baseman who got knocked cold when a peg from the outfield hit him between the eyes. Or a hundred other things that you probably had to be there to truly appreciate.

It didn't occur to me that my teammates might nurture the same memories until I ran into three of them last summer. I don't get back to Salt Lake much anymore, so this was the first time we'd been together in 28 years, and yet our recollections matched perfectly. Maybe too perfectly, because the left-hander in the bunch remembered me telling him to throw the pitch I called for with a game on the line or I'd stick the ball up his ass. He was 6-foot-6 and tough enough to have kept fighting after he broke both hands in a brawl. Most likely the only reason he didn't pinch my head off back then was because we won. He didn't do it now, either, thank God. Instead, he laughed. We all did. Then we moved on to the next memory. When I thought about it later, I realized that we had become old ballplayers ourselves. And it felt as good as I always thought it would.

GQ, April 1996

K48

It was funny how the fight started. Twilight was descending on the ballpark we called Muni, and I was trying to keep a seventh-inning rally going against a right-hander who had washed out of the Florida State League. I took an outside pitch, and when I glanced behind me, I saw the catcher – my friend Dave Disorbio – rubbing the ball in the dirt. He was laughing while the umpire stood there like a dummy.

I started cussing Disorbio, and the ump just shrugged and said he didn't have any other balls. What happened after that should have been triumph enough for a less-than-terrifying hitter who never got paid in more than beer: I lined the next pitch to right for a single. But I kept yapping at Disorbio, and when the final out had been made and my team had lost again, I took the obligatory sprint around the bases and found him waiting at home plate.

The teammates who pulled us apart acted like they had been to a funeral for a friendship. They talked about how we had dipped into the same bag of chewing tobacco and packed each other out of bars. Judging from their mournful tones, not a man among them would have bet his dirtiest pair of sanitary socks that we would ever take batting practice together again. But Disorbio and I were out there the next day, for the bond between us was a bat, and though a good curveball could always get the best of it, a mere fight never would.

We had a sack of beat-up balls and a Little Leaguer named Bobby DiPasquale to shag for us. As I stare out my office window on winter afternoons all these years later, I wish I could go back and take a few more cuts. But Bobby is grown up now, Disorbio has a high school athletic program to run and I'm moving toward a waistline the size of Ted Williams's lifetime batting average. Once youth leaves, it never returns. But I asked my wife to give me a bat for my birthday anyway.

Shielding me from the onset of middle age has become one of her annual projects. A year ago she tracked down albums by the Pretenders and the Cars to get me out of the dark ages musically. This year I gave her a different mountain to climb when I stumbled across an ad for personalized Louisville Sluggers in the back of the *Sporting News*. When she got on the phone to Hillerich & Bradsby, the bat barons, she told the nice lady on the other end of the line that she wanted a K48 model, 34 inches long, 33 ounces in weight. The nice lady told my wife she knew more about bats than most of the big-league *fraus* who call. It was a great scam while it lasted, but my wife ruined it by repeating what I had told her: that the K48 was the bat Babe Ruth used to swing.

"Do you know who Red Kress is?" she asked me after completing a long-distance course in Louisville Slugger lore.

"Doesn't he fight oil-well fires?" I said.

If Red Kress does, he changed his name to Red Adair and never played 14 years in the big leagues; never piled up a .286 career average with the Browns, White Sox, Senators, Tigers, and Giants; and most assuredly never died in 1962. Oh, the shame of not knowing that the K48 was Red Kress's war club while the Babe's was an R43. But I'll tell you what a good sport my wife is: she gave me my bat anyway.

It arrived three weeks after I turned 37, and as soon as I unwrapped it, I stopped griping about the wait. I had never seen my name on a bat before, had scarcely even touched a bat since the last time I grounded out to shortstop, and to tell the truth, I was moved in a way I hadn't expected. Where once I had been a kid with dreams of pounding a double off the short porch in Sportsman's Park in St. Louis, I was now a man recalling how nice it had been to be that kid.

Baseball was a wonderland to me then, and when the first friend I made in Salt Lake City showed me the broken bat he kept in his bedroom, I stared at the name on it for a long time: Lou Vassie. I tried to imagine what Lou Vassie looked like and the way he moved at second base. Never did I suspect that I would one day walk up to Dallas Green, the Cubs' new general manager, and remind him that Lou Vassie was his teammate on the 1956 Salt Lake Bees.

I always had a habit of identifying with obscure ballplayers; maybe it was an unconscious acknowledgment of my own limitations. When Preston Ward forgot who he was and leaped to the top of the American League's hitters in 1958, however briefly, I took his name every time I picked up a bat and started swinging it in front of the mirror in our living room. (My mother didn't approve – something about the fragility of her Danish porcelain, if memory serves.) Next up in my imaginings was Mike White, the pride of Houston for half of the '64 season. Then came Glenn Vaughan, a failed bonus baby who mysteriously lost a bat when he blew into Salt Lake with the Oklahoma City 89ers. By now my wife, friends, fellow literati, and everyone else within shouting distance have heard about them all. My fate is sealed. I'm the nut who got a bat for his birthday.

I can give you the sage advice of a thousand batting coaches: "Don't lounge at the ball." I can imitate Stan Musial's peekaboo stance, the *S* that Gene Woodling curled himself into, and the big swing that always spun the batting helmet off Leon Wagner's head. I have the only prop I need for such grand performances, and I am a happy man. My cup may not runneth over, but my bat rack is full.

Chicago Sun-Times, February 24, 1982

American Legion Summers

Even in the San Fernando Valley, which sometimes feels like the devil's own blast furnace, summer is starting to die. The sun no longer blinds us with its overhand fastball, and the nights have turned blessedly cool. But I'm not enjoying these first hints of autumn as much as I normally would because another facet of summer changed when I didn't want it to. My favorite baseball team played its final game.

Woodland Hills West sounds like a housing development, but in truth it was a juggernaut of kids, most of them 17 and 18, who won the nation's American Legion championship last year and were convinced they could repeat this year. And why not? They had spent June and July rattling off a 21-game winning streak, hadn't they? But two losses in a regional tournament last weekend ended their dreams and their season and left them contemplating far more than summer's end. As first baseman Jason Cohen told the *Los Angeles Times*, "This is the last time I'll get to play with some of my best friends in the world."

His words, forged with purity and perspective, made me realize how lucky I had been to root for a team that didn't count George Steinbrenner as its temporarily deposed owner. Or Jose Canseco as its emotionally undernourished slugger. Or snarling, drunken Philadelphians as the public it could never please. The force that drove Woodland Hills West came not from the ego or the wallet but the heart.

Perhaps I should have realized that, for when I started following West in the local sports section last summer, it was winning the

Legion World Series even though one of its stars had defected and its catcher had torn up his thumb. But it wasn't until I started bicycling to their weekend games a couple of months ago that the source of their strength became apparent. The names in the paper now had faces. And the faces had stories.

Del Marine, whose slugging made him the 1989 Legion Player of the Year, had already been to two junior colleges and tried unsuccessfully to trade his third baseman's glove for a quarterback's playbook. Bobby Kim, who came to this country from Korea six years ago, stood tall as a catcher and clutch hitter while his parents and brothers watched with silent pride. Jason Cohen kept driving in runs without making an all-star team or getting the college scholarship he deserved.

The longer I watched West, the more I thought about my own days of playing Legion ball in Salt Lake City for a tobacco-chewing original named Sheik Caputo. The year was 1963, but I still remember a triple I hit in the state tournament and how a circus catch robbed me of another one. I remember how my team got bounced from the tourney it was supposed to win and how, afterward, Sheik Caputo sat on the bumper of his old Mercury with tears in his eyes as his daughter patted him on the shoulder and said, "That's okay, Dad."

Someday, if time still ages such moments the way it has for me, the kids from Woodland Hills will understand what I am talking about. They will recall this summer as the one that got away, of course, but there will always be something to take the sting off it. Maybe it will be the pride that came with winning two double-headers in two days, or maybe it will be a laugh about the sanitary socks that never got washed when they were on their 21-game tear. And maybe, if they are really lucky, they will still be able to call one another friends.

National Sports Daily, August 24, 1990

Basil

Evening was coming on and the cats were crying for their dinner. There were two of them, and they couldn't understand how I, this stranger who had volunteered to feed them in their masters' absence, could ignore them so studiously. The cold shoulder had something to do with the 1973 World Series flickering on the color television that I never would have been able to watch in my own apartment. But my reasons ran deeper than that, for I wasn't just watching a game. I was looking into my past.

On the surface, it wasn't such a glorious sight, particularly when my exploits as a baseball player came to mind. After all the hours I had spent as a manchild on the dusty diamonds of Salt Lake City, just one moment deserved to be preserved in Kodachrome. It involved a Boston Red Sox scout who came out of the stands the summer before my senior year in high school and, cigar in mouth, said, "You caught a big league game tonight." Unfortunately, I didn't see him again until the day before I went in the army six years later, an occasion he used to smite me with the truth: "Hustle don't hit a curveball."

It was, I have always supposed, the perfect epitaph for a career that produced only a thin scrapbook filled with the residue of meager accomplishments. And yet, as I sat there 2,000 miles from Salt Lake – a dreamy cityside reporter who had come to work in gritty old Baltimore because it was a writers' town – I felt a sudden sense of fulfillment.

On the TV in front of me, the Mets were straining to get something going against Oakland in the fifth inning, and now they were sending up an angular rookie named George Theodore to pinch-hit for Ray Sadecki, the long-in-tooth left-hander. To most, it was just one of the dozens of moves that would be made in an interminable game, a pebble tossed in baseball's ocean. To me, it was everything I had been waiting for since I realized that the World Series was for me to watch, not to play in.

Ray Sadecki was just a face on a bubblegum card and always would be.

But George Theodore was a friend.

We came from a shared experience, and somehow he had succeeded in spite of it. Utah, after all, is hardly a breeding ground for big leaguers. Maybe the blame for that should be hung on the drinking water at the Magna ballpark, water that tasted as though it had just been pumped out of the nearby copper smelter. Or maybe it was the one-watt lighting system at the Sandy ballpark that did in so many of us. But it figured that not every place we played could be as fine as Muni, the outsized park in the heart of Salt Lake that was so lovingly tended by a 5-foot-3 Italian known as "the Tall Swede." The Swede kept rocks out of the infield, sleepy winos out of the dugouts, and his eyes open for hot prospects. "This Theodore," he told me one day, "is really gonna be something."

George was two years my junior – the kid brother of a rival outfielder I had long verbally abused – and he possessed the savvy and skill I would never have. It was this way when we played against each other in high school and American Legion ball and when we found ourselves together on Utah Power & Light's twilight league team. Never was the difference between us more clearly etched than during our brief time in the same lineup. I was just home from graduate school, a never-was of 23 who would quickly move on to a copy editor's job at the *Salt Lake Tribune*. George, on the other hand, kept creating advertisements for himself with line drives. In less time than it took to figure out his batting average, he was on his way to Bellingham, Washington, to play on a team composed of young giants bound for glory.

It would be only fitting if my last in-person memory of George were the cloud of dust he left me in, but that was not his way. Such a parting would have been too serious, too pretentious, and George was nothing if not amiably goofy. That was why teammates and opponents alike called him by his middle name, Basil. Somehow it better suggested what he was: a heavy hitter who had connected with enough books to know that Dal Maxvill wasn't in the same league as Descartes and Daedalus.

Even in high school, Basil sported horn-rimmed glasses and a slightly dazed air on the field and off. It was nothing for someone to get a base hit and perch proudly on first base, only to be jerked into Basil's world when he asked, "Do you really think God is dead?" Theology was just one of his interests, along with astrology, psychology, extrasensory perception, philosophy, nutrition, reincarnation, and poetry. He was maddeningly well rounded, but a cherry-nosed scout for the California Angels thought he had discovered a sticking point when he learned that Basil dabbled in free verse and Elizabethan couplets. "You can't trust a poet," the scout said.

Basil was willing to run the gauntlet of small minds, though. For his daring, he received a contract with the Mets, an organization that feared nothing and no one after surviving Jimmy Piersall and Choo-Choo Coleman. Basil fit in perfectly. As soon as he made it to the majors in '73, he bet a guitar that a team executive couldn't identify the poet who wrote "The Force That Through the Green Fuse Drives the Flower." It was Dylan Thomas, and the executive couldn't.

From what I could tell as I read the newspaper and magazine stories that popped up about Basil, everything was in order. Everything, that is, except his nickname. Somewhere in the minor leagues, a dugout wit apparently had got a load of the way Basil flapped his arms when he ran and how his 180 pounds were strung over a 6-foot-4 frame. And so he became "the Stork," a name some people still insist on calling him. I was dismayed, but I held my silence until he collided with an outfield wall and landed in the hospital with a dislocated hip.

"No more wind sprints, huh?" I said when I called him.

"Only Zen wind sprints."

He was still Basil.

I think that was what made me so happy when I saw him come up to pinch-hit in the second game of the '73 World Series. Until that moment, with him striding through the afternoon shadows in Oakland to face Vida Blue and me cat-sitting in an apartment in Baltimore, I had never known anyone who had gone so far in baseball. If I tell you now that I was thrilled, I will be understating the way I felt.

True, the Series is for thrills. In every October I can recall, beginning with Willie Mays's impossible catch in 1954, there have been memories to save for future generations. I watched from the couch in my parents' home as Sandy Koufax mowed down the Yankees in '63. In my fifth week as a newspaperman in Baltimore, a benevolent city editor assigned me to do crowd stories so I could see Brooks Robinson perform magic. And since I began writing sports five years ago, I have witnessed Reggie Jackson's three homers on three swings and Bucky Dent's taste of greatness and Willie Stargell's tears of joy. But for me, nothing will ever equal the sight of George Basil Theodore, who would be gone from the Mets and the big leagues by the middle of the next season, simply stepping up to the plate.

I wish I could remember if he looked calm or nervous, if he scooped up a handful of dirt or spent a long time studying the third base coach's signals. But everything is a blur because I was on my feet, driving my friends' cats crazy as I leaped around the living room shouting, "All right, Basil! Jesus, I don't believe it! All right! Allllllll riiiiiiight!" The next thing I knew, he had hit an easy ground ball to shortstop for an out.

I slumped in a chair and told myself it didn't matter. Basil had played in the World Series. It was in the record book now: a kid from Salt Lake had made it, a kid I had played with. I sat there for a long time, and when I finally arose, I fed the cats a dinner as magnificent as the occasion.

Sporting News, October 25, 1980

10

Hit and Run

Fans' Notes

Studs Terkel knew about everything else, from the Wobblies to Eudora Welty, so why wouldn't he know about baseball? Wild Bill Hagy drove a cab in Baltimore, so if he hadn't known about baseball, he would have lost his license. But it came as a surprise to learn that rock-and-roll's George Thorogood loved the game so much that he built himself a ballpark. I, on the other hand, was telling myself I was falling out of love with baseball, yet there I was, in a rental car, on an interstate, transported by what I heard on the radio. The players come and go; the true fans are there for the long haul – and no one was ever a truer fan than a doctor from Brooklyn who loved his Dodgers for as long as he possibly could.

Hilly and Garvey

She was there again when the Dodgers returned to Wrigley Field. It was August of last year and the baseball strike was over and maybe she was looking for familiar rocks to lean on. The Dodgers were certainly that, a team she had been bonded to by her husband, and when she peeked into their dugout, she saw Dusty Baker and the familiar warmth returned. He was one of her favorites, and the feeling was mutual.

"Hey, where's your old man?" he asked with that big smile of his. Nancy Abzug swallowed hard. "Didn't Steve Garvey tell you?"

"No."

"Well, Hilly passed away in June."

She still wonders if those were tears in Baker's eyes as he hurried back to the clubhouse without a word. If they were, there couldn't have been a memorial that would have pleased Dr. Hillyard Abzug more, for he loved the Dodgers like few other things in his short, happy life.

They went all the way back to Brooklyn together, back to Ebbets Field and the days of Jackie, Campy, and the Duke. Hilly Abzug was there to suffer at the hands of the hated Yankees through so many Octobers and to dance madly through the streets when there was finally a World Series his Bums could claim as their own. He didn't mind being called irrational. In fact, if anybody neglected to do so, he was perfectly capable of pointing out that when the Dodgers left Brooklyn, he left with them.

Of course, Hilly never went as far as Los Angeles. After undergraduate work at the University of Chicago, there was med school at the same place, and, eventually, he became the director of emergency services at Lutheran General Hospital in Park Ridge – a soft, furry, lovable bear of a man whose blue eyes calmed more than one stretcher case. "When you see a patient in emergency, you have about 30 seconds to get his confidence," Nancy Abzug says, "and Hilly could do it. He was tender and natural and everybody liked him." The only trick he employed to maintain the good feeling was that he never admitted he really wanted to be the Dodgers' team physician.

Since there were too many miles between him and his dream, he settled for ardent fandom. He never went to sleep until he found out how the Dodgers had done, and he pretended the static on his radio didn't exist when he picked up their games with the Braves on an Atlanta station. He bought a condo in Florida so he could go to spring training, and he never missed the Dodgers when they came to Chicago. But that wasn't enough, so he went on the road to catch two more series every season. In the process, his wife decided that the worst peanuts are in Pittsburgh and the best hot dogs are in Montreal, which was a blessing because, with night games, she and Hilly never got out to sample the fabled local cuisine.

It sounds crazy, but the Abzugs were serious about their devotion, and they had the T-shirts to prove it. "I remember the first time I saw Hilly and Nancy," says Steve Garvey, whose father used to drive the Dodgers' team bus in spring training and who grew up to symbolize the team's best qualities. "Their shirts had 'Brooklyn Dodgers' written across the chest, and I told myself, 'I've got to meet those people.'"

Garvey walked over and began a friendship that would thrive for the last six years of Hilly Abzug's life. Wherever their paths crossed, Garvey always had a big hello for them and a baseball and a peck on the cheek for their four daughters. The other Dodgers followed suit, and pretty soon the people sitting around the Abzugs were wondering what the fuss was about. "They'd ask if we were groupies," Nancy says. "Maybe we were." She knows better than that, though.

Away from the ballpark, she and Hilly never got any chummier than breakfast with Garvey's family and a drink with former Dodger coach Jim Lefebvre. They didn't want the Dodgers to think they were imposing; they didn't want to wear on anybody's patience. And yet one of the first people Nancy thought of contacting when Hilly got sick was Garvey. They weren't just his fans by then; they were his friends.

"My husband found out he had cancer in 1979," Nancy says. "He had an operation and he was okay for 10 months and then . . . well, you know. I wrote Steve and the Dodgers a letter telling them that with the kind of cancer Hilly had, he wasn't going to make it. I wanted to ask a favor of them. Hilly had always seen all those people on the field before games, and he wanted to be down there himself. That's all – he just wanted to get on the field. And every time we went to a game after that, there he was. I'm telling you, the Dodgers couldn't have been nicer."

That's the kind of story this is. When Nancy chartered a bus and brought 50 friends to Wrigley Field for a Dodgers-Cubs birthday party for Hilly two years ago, they made sure that Garvey had a T-shirt just like everyone else; it said "Brooklyn Dodgers" on the front and "Hilly's 44th" on the back. And when the end was drawing nigh last June, the voice that brought Hilly back to consciousness one last time belonged to Garvey. "It was sad," the Dodger star says, "but it was an honor, too."

As if to prove it, Garvey still wears Hilly's birthday T-shirt, still says it gives him inspiration, still swears he left the doctor with a deathbed promise of a world championship. No matter where fact ends and fiction begins, it is all too perfect to be tampered with. There could be no better finale for the life of the Brooklyn boy who cherished the Dodgers like family.

Nancy Abzug may have said as much by buying tickets to the Dodgers-Cubs series that opens Friday and getting her best T-shirt ready. When she walks into Wrigley Field, she will be accompanied not only by one of her daughters, but by the memories she built there while her husband was dying. They aren't sad memories, either. They are beautiful, just the way Hilly Abzug was.

Chicago Sun-Times, May 28, 1982

Baseball Blues

There is no thinking about baseball when George Thorogood duck-walks across the stage. He struts his stuff the way Chuck Berry used to, pumping new life into that rowdy genius's old hits, and it's impossible to imagine that there is anything more on his mind than becoming a roadhouse legend himself. But once the music fades and the crowd disappears into the night, the time has come to realize that Thorogood didn't yearn to dress like Ty Cobb on Halloween just because his Dracula costume got lost at the cleaners.

"Man, Ty Cobb was the scariest thing that ever played ball," he says. So what better persona could this wandering second baseman from Delaware adopt if just for one night? It matters not that he has an album called *Bad to the Bone* roaring up the charts or that he and his band, the Destroyers, are packing clubs and cow palaces alike on their national tour. Thorogood's vision of paradise remains unchanged. All he asks are up-to-the-minute World Series scores from stagehands and a little reverence for baseball when the grass was real.

He nurtures a passion for the game that mystifies the rock writers who come to trace his ties to Howlin' Wolf, Willie Dixon, and all the other blues masters. They want to find out if 29-year-old George Thorogood is haunted by the same demons that shoved Robert Johnson into an early grave, and his answers make sense only to those among them who remember that the illustrious Hank Aaron got traded back to Milwaukee for lusterless Davey May.

Maybe that isn't fair, because Thorogood spent his formative years as a batboy for a semipro team that had not only May in its lineup, but May's brother Scrappy as well. The truth of the matter, however, is that Thorogood's enthusiasm encompasses more than mere trivia. He can be a wiseacre about his favorite team: "How big a Mets' fan am I? Oh, about 5–10." And he can be an unrepentant traditionalist when he bemoans the passing of Philadelphia's ancient Connie Mack Stadium: "I look at the parks they've got now, these places that look like community centers, and I say, 'Jesus, is this what Jackie Robinson suffered for?'"

The more you listen to Thorogood, the more you realize why he makes a point of wearing one of Bernie Carbo's castoff Cardinal jerseys in pickup games. If he ever earns a gold record, he wants to pick it up at Shea Stadium with the Mets looking on. If he ever met a big leaguer he liked as much as Carbo, it was Bill Lee, the interplanetary left-hander who refused to stop thinking of baseball as something more than a plaything for the idle rich. If he ever had a better time at a ballpark than he does watching Fenway Park's Green Monster get shelled, it was in 1979, when he trotted out to second base for his own ball club – the Destroyers, fittingly.

"I don't know if I can explain how I felt," Thorogood says. "There I was in our first game of the season, standing on a real diamond, wearing a real uniform. And I wasn't just sitting on the bench; I was starting. I got a hit my first time up, the only hit we got all game, but that wasn't why it meant so much to me. I hadn't played on a team since I was 12, and being out there was like, man, it was like finding religion."

To take the metaphor two steps further, Thorogood's church was the Roberto Clemente League, and his pew was of his own making. He had never been good enough to play anywhere beyond Little League, and he had given up hope of doing so until the money started coming in from *George Thorogood and the Destroyers*, his first and, to at least one listener's ears, best album. Then he started to visualize the fantasy he would live. He pictured a team called the Destroyers and the ballpark he would build for them and the classic uniforms he would dress them in – "real old-time flannels, not that double-knit crap." Everything was just so in his dream, and it turned out to be the same in reality until he was waylaid by success.

For openers, he was the Clemente League's rookie of the year, and his Destroyers finished second. The next season, he batted .300, and they reigned as champions. "Forget about my average," says Thorogood, like a good team man. "Just tell the people we won everything." The Destroyers did it in high style, too, yelling, "Move it on over!" every time they got a runner on base. The uninitiated had to figure out for themselves that the Destroyers' war cry was also the title of one of their second baseman's favorite songs.

But that was in 1980, and the Destroyers – the ball club, not the band – haven't been anything except also-rans since then. Blame it on the summer tour that the Destroyers – the band, not the ball club – took with the Rolling Stones a year ago. Or blame it on the album that now has them bouncing from Des Moines to Minneapolis to Chicago like a double off the wall.

"I know what's happening," Thorogood says. "I don't call home every day and all that Charlie Finley stuff, but I'm part owner, so I've got ways of finding out what's going on, you know what I mean? Soon as we get off the road, I'm going to put the hammer down. Our manager went and got married, and his wife got pregnant, and all that miserable stuff. Man, some people just don't care enough about baseball."

They don't wish Ebbets Field were still standing, and they can't close their eyes and see Ted Williams turning out the lights on another pitcher. They don't remember how Duke Snider looked as a Met, and they don't cherish the past. "Sometimes I wish baseball was the way it was when those old-time cats were playing," Thorogood says. "You know, they rode trains, and they made about 18 grand a year, and they blew all their money on booze and broads." But that train pulled out of the station long ago, never to return, and all one particular second baseman can do about it is what he does best – sing the blues.

Chicago Sun-Times, November 5, 1982

A Mischievous Eye on Time

When Studs Terkel looks at baseball, he sees America's face. The sight comes complete with an eclectic text – prose by William Saroyan and Nelson Algren, poetry by Edgar Allen Poe, song lyrics by Leadbelly. But at the very root of it all is the memory of the ballplaying bus driver who used to carry Studs to his callings as author and actor, musicologist and sociologist, oral historian and Chicago legend. In the summer, the bus driver was as single-minded as Studs was, and is, many-faceted. All he thought about was base hits.

"How'd you do yesterday?" Studs would ask on Monday mornings.

"Line drives, nothing but sweet line drives," the driver would reply.

Or: "Not so hot. Beat out a bunt is all. Pitcher was tough. Ooohwee, was he tough."

Good performance or bad, though, the driver was imbued with an unrelenting passion for his sport, a boundless love for a game that belongs on green grass under a cloudless sky. Studs Terkel could appreciate that. "Don't get me wrong now," he says. "I was never a player or anything like that. I've always been a spectator, a fan. But the way this man loved baseball, I'm telling you, it set something off in me." And when that happened, the clock inside Studs's head started spinning backward.

It wouldn't stop until he could picture himself just after the scandal-scarred 1919 World Series, 7 years old and puzzled by the hubbub over what the Black Sox had done. Not until later would he get together with the brilliantly dyspeptic Algren to curse Charlie

Comiskey as a penurious owner and bemoan Shoeless Joe Jackson and Buck Weaver as victims of circumstance, not greed. In the beginning, the child who was born Louis Terkel simply prayed that the game would find a savior, never suspecting that it would discover one as great or perplexing as George Herman Ruth.

"I've got this theory about the Babe," Studs says. "I think the baseball owners hated him just like the big shots hated Roosevelt. Sure, the New Deal got the economy going again and the Babe's home runs saved baseball, but – I've got this theory – Ruth and Roosevelt made all those guys who thought they were powerful aware of their own mortality. God, I'll bet they hated that."

Studs laughs so hard that he has to take his cigar out of his mouth lest he swallow it. "You enjoying this?" he asks. The speed at which his memory is traveling doesn't give him time to wait for an answer.

While standing in Chicago, he is back in his birthplace, back in the Bronx, back where he fell for the New York Giants. "Nobody liked the Yankees," he says. "They were like the Dodgers are now – show biz." He makes a face and doesn't let it go until the conversation shifts to Frankie Frisch, the Fordham Flash. "Solid, never did the wrong thing," Studs says. "I guess he was the best player I ever saw." Or does that honor belong to the Babe, even if he was a Yankee? Or Ty Cobb? Or Satchel Paige? Or Paul Waner? "Paul Waner was on the juice, you know." But does that mean he wasn't better than Carl Hubbell? Or Lefty Grove? Or Willie Mays? "Nothing wrong with Willie Mays," says Studs.

He has seen them all, soaked up their greatness with the same mischievous eyes that watched the last game the St. Louis Browns ever played. To him, baseball is a way to tell time, to mark periods in your life. Take the first time he ever got hustled. It was 1925, his mother had just moved to Chicago to open a boarding house, and he was watching the play-by-play of the World Series being flashed on one of those old-time headline scoreboards.

"All of a sudden this kid leans out of a window above me and says, 'I'll bet you a nickel Buddy Myer gets a hit,'" Studs recalls. "See, Buddy Myer had just replaced Bucky Harris at second for the

Senators. So I figure the guy's cold, he hasn't warmed up yet, and I take the bet." Studs turns the cigar in his mouth over slowly. "The kid had a crystal set up there; he knew what happened before they showed it on the scoreboard. I didn't find that out until he had my nickel."

In the long run, of course, Studs was the winner, the proud owner of a story that underscores what he calls baseball's most important product – delight. Small wonder, then, that he reveres Bill Veeck, owner of the White Sox, founder of the exploding scoreboard, and erstwhile employer of a pinch-hitting midget. "Even if Veeck's team loses," Studs says, "he's still going to give you something to remember."

The Cubs, on the other hand, have given Studs nothing but moments to forget. "They're a bourgeois team," he says. For proof, he offers everything from Jolly Cholly Grimm's stand against black players to the frat-house behavior of Wrigley Field's bleacher dwellers.

"They've got their beer and they boo each other," he says, "but they don't know what the hell's going on. I remember one time I was out there and Ron Santo struck out. So now Billy Williams or Ernie Banks, one of them, was up and the count was a ball and a strike or something, and the kid next to me – he's got a transistor radio pressed against his ear – he says, 'Santo just struck out.' 'How do you know?' I ask him. He says, 'The announcer said so.'"

What better explanation for why Studs cleaves to the past so tenaciously? In the past, the ballplayers were more than automatons. It meant something to see King Carl Hubbell and Prince Hal Schumacher throw a pair of 1–0 games at the Dean brothers or to stop by a newsstand and find out that Edd Roush had hit a homer for Cincinnati. But come the change in eras, Bill Wambsganss, who made the only unassisted triple play in World Series history, wrote a fan letter to Studs saying, "You probably don't remember me."

The hell Studs didn't.

Chicago Sun-Times, July 2, 1980

Wild Bill

He is big, very big, but what should we use as the definitive measure?
The question, remember, is box office, not bulk. So forget about
dragging out your bathroom scale and your stale jokes about how
he passed 200 pounds several dozen cases of beer ago. The trusty old
yardstick can stay put, too, even though it proves that he stands 6-
foot-3 with no help whatsoever from his hairless noggin. If we are to
understand our subject at all, then maybe this is the best way to size
him up: nobody on the Baltimore Orioles is doing a TV commercial,
and Wild Bill Hagy is.

"I don't understand it," says one Oriole.

And another.

And another.

Perhaps when they finish hashing things out with the Pirates in
the World Series, this Greek chorus of chagrin will take a good look
at where it is. Only Baltimore could cleave to a cab driver who
twists his roly-poly body this way and that to spell out the home
team's name. In any other city, Wild Bill would be just another crazy
flirting with a night in the hoosegow. But fate delivered him here,
where the sleaziest strip joint on the infamous Block is treated with
reverence and the newspaper files on racetrack touts are thicker
than those on cancer research at Johns Hopkins University. Give
Wild Bill credit for an unerring sense of place.

He gets the most attention when he is on the roof of the Orioles'
dugout. He clambers up there in the middle of every seventh inning
– assisted by an usher, no less – and leads the Memorial Stadium

crowd in his famous cheer: "o-r-i-o-l-e-s!" The joint is rocking, and down in the dugout, the objects of his affection are talking.

"They're amazed," Wild Bill says. "I tell 'em there ain't anything that amazing about it. They could do the same if they drank a case of beer every night."

The exposure has worked wonders for Wild Bill no matter what his level of sobriety. "I was out in Anaheim for the playoffs," he says. "I musta signed a couple thousand autographs." No surprise there, for nary a network camera crew or wire service photographer has failed to draw a bead on him. The attention has made Wild Bill a celebrity, and celebrities attract their peers – Pee Wee Reese, Howard Cosell, Willie Stargell. "Did you hear what Stargell told me?" Wild Bill asks. "He said I was doing a great job and to keep it up." The memory of those words lights up a vintage smile, one that reveals his missing front tooth. A prominent Baltimore dentist has promised to replace it for free. That's how big Wild Bill is.

"I never thought I'd meet 90 percent of the people I know now," he says. He isn't exaggerating. The people he knows now are hardly the kind you find in section 34 of Memorial Stadium's upper deck, where he usually hangs his battered straw cowboy hat. Instead, the cast of characters includes a sweet young thing who, in tamer circles, might be called an exhibitionist and a gentleman who talks to squirrels and calls himself Derf. "Derf," says Wild Bill, "is Fred spelled backwards."

In their midst, Wild Bill looms as an unlikely father figure. When all this started in 1972, he was just another hack from the North Point Cab Company, just another bowler who did his drinking at Ed's Inn, in the blue-collar stronghold of Dundalk. There were no more than 20 regulars in the section then, and Wild Bill was trying to pick up bar money by stocking the ballpark's beer cooler after games. He might still be doing it if he hadn't accidentally locked himself in the cooler overnight. It was too cold in there for him to do any serious drinking, but local historians insist that doesn't matter. The legend of Wild Bill Hagy was born.

He added to it in 1977, when he loaded his cab with a few loaded friends and drove to Cleveland to watch the Orioles' final game of the season. Even that expedition, however, has been overwhelmed by this season's infernal combustion.

Wild Bill beseeches section 34's 2,000 converts in a voice that sounds like a cement mixer in action, waving his hat madly and waiting for the Orioles' management to acknowledge him. At present there can only be speculation as to what took the Orioles so long. Maybe they were put out by the fact that Wild Bill's gang brings its own beer to the park in coolers rather than pay the vendors' inflated prices. Or maybe they were offended by the number of times the regulars failed to make it all the way to the restroom. Whatever, when one of Wild Bill's admirers suggested that the management announce the great man's 40th birthday on the stadium scoreboard, the response was the ultimate insult: "How do you spell his name?"

Now the Orioles know. They read it in the Baltimore papers. They read it in the *New York Times*. They read it every time they turn around. They know that he has been married almost as often as Elizabeth Taylor, and that he spent half a dozen years as a Good Humor man, and that their wisest move was to buy him a round-trip ticket to California for the playoffs. The moral: You don't mess around with someone as big as Wild Bill Hagy.

"Did you see me on *The Great Baltimore Baffle*?" he asks. He is sitting in Ed's Inn, a beer in each hand, warming up for the night ahead. "Oh, I forgot, you're from out of town. Well, *The Great Baltimore Baffle* is this quiz show they got on TV here. They said they had more mail than ever before when I was a panelist there."

The most, the best, the biggest, the hottest – Wild Bill has a hand in them all. One night he is picking up $200 for a personal appearance at a Pontiac dealer, the next he is earning $500 for the Chevrolet commercial the Oriole players think should be theirs. And now he has just returned from providing some background noise for a locally produced disco record. "Yeah, yeah, I know," he says wearily. "Section 34's supposed to be against disco. But what the hell, ain't no sense in short-changing myself now."

He pauses to knock back one of his beers. When he pulls the can away from his mouth, the look on his face suggests P. T. Barnum after he sold his first ticket to a snipe hunt.

"Hey," says Wild Bill Hagy, "do you think I should get me an agent?"

Chicago Sun-Times, October 16, 1979

On the Road to Sioux Falls

Rain was starting to fall, its drops spreading across the windshield of my rented car like fat, wet bugs. The sky to the west was as forbidding as a state trooper's scowl. "Snow tonight," said a voice on the radio. I punched up a different station and found something that didn't make a springtime Sunday afternoon seem like a bad joke – baseball.

They were only talking about it on the Kansas City Royals' network, but that was good enough for me. I could hear batting practice pitches being whacked this way and that in the background, and if someone was taking batting practice, a game couldn't be far behind. So let them talk if they wanted to. Baseball is as much a game of words as it is of deeds.

First there was a replay of the home run George Brett had hit the night before, the home run that made him the Royals' all-time leader. Then there was the inevitable question. "It's only because I've been playing so long," Brett answered, laughing.

It was the kind of self-effacing response we like from our heroes, and yet the longer I dwelled on what he had said, the more I was distracted by other things. Like Brett's soft drawl. When did a kid who grew up among surfers in Southern California start sounding like he had come of age in a country band aiming for the Grand Ole Opry? And where did I get off calling him a kid? George Brett is 32 – he said so himself – and that is simply an age I used to be, which no doubt was part of my problem.

I punched the dial again.

This time it was the Minnesota Twins coming to me courtesy of a hinterland station whose wattage I would outdistance as soon as I went over the next hill. The Twins are largely strangers these days; for every Hrbek, there is a Lombardozzi. But the play-by-play of their game filled me with good feelings anyway, because it brought back memories that really had nothing to do with them. They were just on the radio – Harmon Killebrew, Mudcat Grant, and that bunch from the mid-'60s – as the beer-league team I played for headed home to Salt Lake City from a weekend series in Worland, Wyoming. We were traveling in three cars, each trying to stay ahead of the others, each trying to shock the others to the back of the pack. And I have to say that the bare rear end protruding from one of the windows provided the necessary shock.

"Looks like Starchy," someone said.

Starchy was our left fielder.

"Either you get him a bar of soap," someone else said, "or you get me a blindfold."

It is hard for me to believe that you can enjoy such lofty conversation when there is a ballgame on television. No wonder I like traveling by car so much during baseball season. No wonder I have such an intense dislike of the cable stations that thrust the Chicago Cubs and the Atlanta Braves into faraway places where baseball would be better off on radio, providing a little mystery and a backdrop for the human comedy.

I suppose that stamps me as a budding old-timer, but there is nothing I can do about it unless I lie about my age. When I was a kid in Los Angeles, I really did hear the Hollywood Stars' broadcaster pronounce Dick Stuart's name "Stir-ut." And I remember how that same golden-throated gent always talked about the aroma that wafted into Seals Stadium, in San Francisco, from the bakery across the street. And I haven't turned off my radio since.

Though evidence to the contrary is embarrassingly abundant, I would like to think this makes me somehow superior to the infidels of the cable age, for radio is a cerebral medium just as baseball is a cerebral sport. To hear it properly, you have to be able to imagine the setting, the stars, and the strategy. Maybe you also have to be able to make things a little better than they are. After all, what good is it to know that the neighborhood around Yankee Stadium is as deadly as a minefield? If you have only your radio and your ears to rely on, the stadium can remain as pure as DiMaggio gliding toward the monuments to turn a triple into an out.

This is hardly my little secret, of course. It belongs, rather, to towns such as Galesburg, Illinois, where one of the local radio stations carried the Rangers' games when native son Jim Sundberg was catching for Texas. And it belongs to a generation that once devoted entire days to playing Strat-O-Matic baseball and now wheels and deals in various rotisserie leagues. Think of how perfect Tim McCarver's imitation of Harry Caray is: "Stan Mew-see-ul stepping to the plate." *Mew-see-ul,* just the way Harry used to say it on the Cardinal broadcasts that McCarver listened to when he was growing up in Memphis.

The Cards ruled the South then, but their signal wasn't beamed in that direction alone. Out in Salt Lake, there was a dentist, the father of a friend of mine, who could get their games only on his car radio. So there he sat, night after night, ignoring the static and never imagining that his dreams would be harpooned in 1963 by a palindromic Dodger named Dick Nen.

But when Nen hit his home run into the famous short porch in St. Louis – Mew-see-ul territory, if you will – I rejoiced, for the Dodgers were my team. They had captured my imagination when they still played in Brooklyn. I lived in Los Angeles long enough to see their first game there, and I spent many a summer night listening to their games come scratching over the mountains after I moved to Salt Lake. As a reward for such loyalty, I got to hear my all-time favorite interview.

Sweet Lou Johnson, who escaped a life in the bushes to provide the '65 Dodgers with almost all of their muscle, had just hit a game-winning homer. Now Jerry Doggett, the second banana to Vin Scully, was asking him to reveal his innermost thoughts.

"Everything gonna be all right, Jerry," said Sweet Lou.

"Fine," Doggett said. "Now what about your homer?"

"Everything gonna be all right."

"What kind of pitch did you hit?"

"Everything gonna. . . ."

There were other nights, however, when I didn't make it past the fifth or sixth inning. I should have had more respect for the brilliance of Scully, who can turn simple play-by-play into a tone poem, but I was young and foolish and sleepy. Sometimes I could sense my mother slipping into my bedroom to turn off the radio. Sometimes I would awaken in the morning to the static of a station I could hear only when the moon was up.

Funny how even that should have seemed special as I searched for baseball on my car radio Sunday, but it did. While speeding toward a future that I can't quite bring into focus, I was captivated by a past when I delighted in such uncertainty. The best pictures I had of Ted Williams's perfect swing, Herb Score's laser-beam fastball, and a host of other wonders were the pictures etched in my imagination.

To tell the truth, it was better that way.

Philadelphia Daily News, April 15, 1986

11

Morman's Mission

Sometimes it feels like baseball dares you to love it. That's the part they don't tell you about when they hand you that first bonus check. They don't tell you that 15 years later you could find yourself in Charlotte on a Saturday night, with a head full of the hits you should have had and the image of Greg Maddux taunting you from the TV in the visitors' clubhouse.

In the right-field pavilion at Knights Stadium, the Famous Chicken is clowning around with a flock of screaming kids, and you're down here with the Durham Bulls wondering if you have stripped the gears in your swing. It is a minor league life in a world that cares only for the majors, a life long on frustration and short on rewards, and you have to love it deep in your soul to stay at it this long. You have to love it the way Russ Morman does.

He has carried the torch for baseball from Glens Falls, New York, to Hawaii, up to Edmonton and down to the Dominican, and now back to an old tobacco town with the team that was immortalized in *Bull Durham*. Kevin Costner played the movie's hero, Crash Davis, a star-crossed wanderer whose past was strewn with home runs, just the way Morman's is. When Morman arrived in Durham this spring, imaginations didn't have to soar very high before the Bulls' new slugger was christened Crash. All Morman asked for in return was the uniform bearing his lucky number, 45. It seemed an easy request to fill until he discovered that at 6-foot-4 and 235 pounds, he would have split the jersey's seams. So he took number 27 without complaint, and the kind hearts and gentle people in Durham knew that this is a man built to pull a heavy load.

At first glance the burden doesn't seem to have worn on Morman. For someone who has squinted in so much afternoon sunshine and frowned at so many bad breaks, his countenance remains remarkably free of crags and crow's feet. It's no exaggeration to call him boyish looking, even at 36. But then there are his eyes, looking for something he will never find in the Triple A International League. His eyes are where the hard times show.

They are showing them now in Charlotte, and who would have thought that could happen here? This is where he prospered the last three seasons – never an average under .314, a personal best 33 homers in '97, and Tommy John, the team's radio color man, joking that the ballpark should be renamed the Morman Tabernacle. But in his return, as Durham's designated hitter, Morman has come up empty. So he stands in the clubhouse, a towel around his waist and an 0-for-4 weight on his shoulders, and he thinks of the two hits he might have had to help the Bulls win. One was a line drive, the other a flare, and both wound up as outs. "You needed those balls to sit down for you," a sympathizer tells him. A moment passes before Morman says, "I know" – and all the air goes out of him.

Then he stares across the room at the TV, where it's still Atlanta at Houston and Maddux doing his old soft-shoe. The sound is off, and the silence makes the big leagues seem further away than they already are.

§ She was still Loretta Ragan when she flew into Buffalo to spend that weekend with Russ. Their first stop was the ballpark, of course, but the game and what he did in it have long since been forgotten. The only thing they remember is how he bounded out of the dugout afterward and motioned her down to the screen separating the field from the box seats. "I got called up," he said. "I'm going to the big leagues."

It was August 2, 1986, and nothing like this had ever happened to him before. The White Sox had lost first baseman Greg Walker with a broken hand, and they needed Russ in their lineup the next day at Comiskey Park. He wanted Loretta to be there with him. Typical

Russ. They were going to be married two days after Thanksgiving, and the sentimental side of him said they should have this memory to share for all their days together.

But they would have only one chance at it, the chance that was beckoning now. So after she dropped him off at Buffalo International at seven o'clock on Sunday morning, Loretta set out for Chicago in his Chevy Blazer, racing the clock and wondering what would happen when she got there. "I didn't have any idea how to get to the ballpark," she says.

Somewhere in Indiana, she stopped hoping she could make it by the first pitch and started twirling the radio dial. She found the game on a Detroit station – the Tigers versus the White Sox – and she heard what happened when right-hander Randy O'Neal threw Russ a 3–2 fastball in his first major league at bat: single up the middle. Loretta screamed for joy and rapturously pounded the steering wheel. The other drivers out there on I-90 could stare all they wanted. The boy she had fallen in love with back home in Independence, Missouri, was making the big time.

It was even better where Russ was, watching the ball he had hit get tossed into the White Sox dugout for safekeeping. The ball he hit his next time up became a keepsake, too. It was a home run off O'Neal that touched down in the left-field stands. "As it was leaving," Russ recalls, "I was thinking, Oh, please don't go in the upper deck. If you hit it in the upper deck, the fans are going to expect that every time." He got his lower-deck wish – and in the same inning, he pounded another base hit.

Loretta heard it all on the Blazer's radio. Then she caught a break of her own on this perfect afternoon as I-90 turned into Chicago's Dan Ryan Expressway, and the Dan Ryan led her straight through the South Side to Comiskey. She rushed into the ballpark in the seventh inning, just in time to see Russ fly out in his last at bat. But nobody in the crowd seemed to care. "I got a standing ovation," he says, and he sounds as amazed and thrilled by it today as he was back then.

The surprises didn't end there, though. In the clubhouse afterward a media mob was waiting to anoint Russell Lee Morman as a hero for the day. "I'd never seen more than one reporter at a time in the minors," he says, "and now I had eight or 10 guys around my locker." They came bearing the news that he had claimed a piece of history: he was the first player since the Yankees' Billy Martin in 1950 to get two hits in one inning in his first big league game. "And I'm standing there going, 'Huh? Are you sure?'"

There was so much to tell Loretta, and no time to do it. She and Russ had barely embraced before he had to board a bus to the airport with the rest of the White Sox. As she watched baseball carry him off for the second time in less than 12 hours, all she could think was, Wow, I guess this is what it's like.

When Russ got to his hotel room in Boston that night, the message light was blinking. Al Michaels wanted to interview him before the *Monday Night Baseball* telecast. Tomorrow he would be facing Roger Clemens. Sleep hardly seemed necessary. He was already in a dream.

§ The merciless future began unfolding in 1988. Three times that year the White Sox called Russ up from Vancouver, and twice they sent him back down. Loretta felt as if she spent the whole summer driving through Montana, usually by herself, because her husband had to fly to a game at whatever his next stop was. The one time they got brave in Chicago, the one time they told themselves he couldn't possibly get shipped out again, they rented an apartment near some of the other Sox instead of playing it safe in a hotel. After they spent their first night there, the big club lowered the boom once more.

It's a wonder that Russ and Loretta ever got out to a movie. But they did, on an off day in Chicago, and what they saw was *Bull Durham*, which is both a love letter to baseball, the minors in particular, and a reminder that God doesn't always give with both hands. Costner's Crash Davis loves the game with a passion it doesn't come close to returning, and Tim Robbins's Nuke LaLoosh treats the great gift of his right arm as if he found it in a box of Cracker Jack. "I remember walking out of the theater feeling sorry for Kevin Costner," Loretta says. "It was like, gosh, he never really got a chance." All Russ knew was that he would buy *Bull Durham* as soon as it came out on video. He wanted to see it again because whoever did it got it right, the laughter and the raunchiness, the toughness and the vulnerability and, yes, the anger too.

There was a reason for that. Ron Shelton, who wrote and directed the movie, had lived the life, working his way up through the Baltimore Orioles' farm system for five seasons, getting as high as Rochester in the International League, playing second base alongside a shortstop named Bobby Grich. But when it was Grich who got the call to take over at second in Baltimore, Shelton knew that baseball was hustling him toward the exit.

He went reluctantly, and even now, 26 years removed from the game and firmly dug in at the plate in Hollywood, he makes no bones about which of his two callings has the greater claim on his soul. "Someday I may win an Academy Award," he says, "but it will never mean as much to me as some of the things I did in baseball." One night in Reno – this would have been '68, the California League – a pitcher who was too dumb to slide barreled into second standing up and broke Shelton's hand. "But I wasn't coming out until I got to hit against the son of a bitch," he says. "And when I did, I almost undressed him with a line drive."

That was how he had been taught to approach the game, and that is how Crash approaches it in the movie as he bounces from one whistle-stop to another with his bat, his catcher's gear and his memories of his 21 days in the Show. "No matter how the game dumped on him," Shelton says, "he remained devoted to it and to the joy of playing it right."

Shelton could just as easily be talking about Russ Morman, though he has never met him and, truth be told, doesn't recognize the name. The similarities between Russ and Crash can be traced all the way to their home runs. The flesh-and-blood slugger pulled into Durham this season with 194 of them, more than any other active minor leaguer. In the movie it is left to Susan Sarandon's beguiling Annie Savoy, a lover of both the game and its most fortunate sons, to point out that Crash has 227 minor league homers when he joins the Bulls. Twenty more and he'll set a record. (Actually, he wouldn't have come close to Hector Espino's minor league standard of 484, but that's not the point.)

"Two hundred and forty-seven home runs in the minor leagues would be kind of a dubious honor," Crash tells Annie. The sentiment is camouflage for his well-earned pride, but Crash is too much of a hardnose to admit it. The man who created him isn't. "There are triumphs in this age of celebrity and hype that are completely unacknowledged," Shelton says. "I happen to think that hitting more home runs in the minors than anybody else means something." It's important to remember that, whether the subject is Crash Davis or Russ Morman.

§ Amtrak number 79 rolls south through Durham late every afternoon, its lonesome whistle and clacking wheels a perfect complement to a three-year-young ballyard that was built to look old. You can see the train if you look past the Blue Monster in left field, although the eyes tend to stop at the large wooden bull perched atop that 32-foot-high fence. Home run hitters win a steak if they hit the bull, or a salad if they only reach the patch of grass painted beneath it. Mercifully, Durham Bulls Athletic Park has enough other nostalgic grace notes to earn forgiveness for its salads and to forestall any yearning for its rickety predecessor, which sits across town, consigned to ghosts and a women's professional softball team. There are nooks and crannies laced with red brick and mementos from the town's lusty past in baseball's outer reaches. Nothing, however, is quite so evocative as the sound of that train when the shadows are growing long.

It harks back to a time before computers and research parks, a time when the now defunct Durham & Southern was hauling what men grew in the rich North Carolina soil. It speaks, too, of the game's essential restlessness, the ebb and flow of players and their dreams. The season was barely into its second month when the big club in Tampa reached out to the Bulls for a third baseman with

10 quick homers and a base-stealing outfielder with wings on his heels. "That's what we're here for," Morman says. "We're not playing to stay in the minors."

There was a time when Morman was the one summoned first, a time when he had the clout of the $75,000 bonus that the White Sox used to lure him out of Wichita State as a junior after drafting him in the first round in 1983. In 1985, after 2 1/2 seasons as a pro, he moved up to Triple A, where he bashed six homers for Buffalo in his first week and started wondering if his goals hadn't been too modest. "I had a timetable for five years," he says. "If I wasn't a major league player by then, that would be it." A rueful smile. "Needless to say, I didn't stick to the timetable very well."

Things started to bog down less than a month after Morman arrived in Chicago with such a clatter in '86. Soon he found himself being platooned at first base. Only time would tell him that his best shot at being a regular in the Show was already history. "You always wonder what Russ would have done if he'd ever had a manager give him 500 at bats in a season," says John Boles, his manager at Buffalo and now the Florida Marlins' director of player development. "Personally, I thought he could be a .280, 25 home run guy."

The rub, as Morman points out, is this: "I don't know if I even have 500 at bats for my whole career in the big leagues."

He doesn't. The exact number is 470, spread over bits and pieces of nine seasons in Kansas City, Florida and, of course, Chicago. All he has to show for those sporadic chances as a first baseman and an outfielder are 10 homers, 43 RBIs and a .249 lifetime batting average – hardly earthshaking statistics, but still more pleasing to the eye than the rejection notices he began receiving in 1989.

That was when the White Sox became the first team to give up on him. He went out the door with but one homer all that season, a brace on his sprained right knee and a new and unwelcome status as a seven-year minor league free agent. Being a free agent in the minors puts the player in the same boat as every blue-collar worker who ever saw a factory go belly up and every middle manager who ever got downsized. It turns him into a supplicant who must do what Morman has done again and again these past nine years: hope that another organization wants him and accept however little it is willing to pay.

The Royals were the first to reach out to Morman, largely at the urging of Boles, who had moved into their front office, and third base coach Smokey Garrett, who had managed Morman when he broke in at Glens Falls. "Russ was a great kid," says Garrett, now in his fourth season as Charlotte's hitting coach. "He became a great man." One the Royals could trust to take a craftsman's diligence to their Omaha farm team, one who wouldn't become just another burnout stuck in Triple A, one whose answer to every problem was to keep plugging away.

Morman was much better than that. When the 1990 Triple A playoffs rolled around, he put Omaha on his broad back and carried it to a championship. "Every time we needed something, he'd come up and hit a homer," says Sal Rende, his manager there as well as at Appleton, Edmonton and Charlotte. And Morman was still on a tear when he arrived at Kansas City's training camp early the next spring. He came to take a whack at catching, an experiment based on the theory that versatility adds to value. He left as the Royals' fourth outfielder and wound up platooning at first base after George Brett, their aging legend, went on the disabled list. "That," Morman says, "was the only time I ever made a big league team out of spring training."

He and Loretta were fresh from buying their first home, in Blue Springs, Missouri, 15 minutes east of Royals Stadium, and their daughter, Katelyn, had just turned one. For once, everything seemed right with their world. Maybe that should have been a warning. But they never saw trouble coming until Loretta looked up at the stadium's message board less than a month into the season and read that Kansas City had just traded for Carmelo Martinez, a veteran power hitter and, alas, a first baseman. "It made me sick," Loretta says. "I knew right then that Russ wasn't going to get his chance."

The pain intensified when they learned that neither manager

John Wathan nor his coaches had lobbied for the trade. It was strictly a front-office maneuver, a deal hatched by men who wear suits instead of uniforms. "We were overruled," Garrett says, "but that's baseball."

It only got worse after that. The Royals released Morman, and he went to spring training in 1992 with Cincinnati, only to have the Reds cut him before they headed north. At first it seemed a blessing that he could be home for the birth of his son, Sam, a thrill he had missed with Katie by half an hour. But after eight weeks of silence, he feared that his career had reached its expiration date. "I was ready to stop hitting and throwing and running," he says. And then the Reds finally called back. They needed his big bat on their Triple A team in Nashville. The catch was, they would pay him only $5,000 a month instead of the $8,000 his original contract called for.

Morman took what they offered. He always does. Without rancor or spite, he signs the contracts that are the bane of the minor league free agent and returns to the game that has a claim on his life. "I've played for as low as $25,000 a year," he says. "It was only a couple of years ago that I finally made $100,000." But that was just once, when the Florida Marlins summoned him as a fifth outfielder at mid-season in '96. The rest of the time his paycheck has been no more than half that for doing something that might have paid him millions if he had only caught a break or been born with the ability to hit his longest balls 10 feet farther.

And still Morman has plugged away in the tradition of Joe Hauser and Stout Steve Bilko and all the other storied minor league sluggers who traveled this trail of tears before him. Since his 30th birthday, he has batted .310 at Nashville in '92, .320 in a return engagement in Buffalo in '93 and .350 at Edmonton the following year – and then came those three lustrous seasons at Charlotte. "Guess I'm a late bloomer," he says.

It was that or be gone, and he has steeled himself against the latter since his final days with the White Sox. He settled under the wing of hitting coach Walt Hriniak and soaked up the wisdom of another man whose playing career forever flirted with extinction.

"Walt always preached that you've got to keep playing until they tear the uniform off you," he says. "As long as you have a uniform on, you still have a chance." If Morman didn't believe that, he wouldn't be in Durham.

§ There have been bad times that somehow gained a certain charm, such as the summer of '87 in Hawaii when Russ hurt his ankle trying to break up a beanball brawl. With only themselves to entertain in those child-free days, he and Loretta wound up visiting all the out-of-the-way beaches they had ever seen on *Magnum, P.I.*

And then there have been times that didn't seem funny until they were over, like the year Loretta and the kids arrived in Edmonton to discover that Russ had unknowingly rented an apartment over a karaoke bar. He had seen it only during the day, but the bar didn't open until night.

And then there have been times that were pure magic, like the day last season when, with Loretta and Katie videotaping everything, Sam got to be Charlotte's batboy and Russ toasted the occasion by hitting two home runs. "Sam was just this little stick figure running around the park picking up bats," Russ says. "He had his sweatbands on and an oversized helmet, and when I crossed the plate after my homers, he was waiting to high-five me."

But mostly it has been Russ by himself in another strange town and Loretta back home in Blue Springs, holding things together until school is out and she and the kids can leave for their two-month summer sojourn with Daddy. This spring Russ missed Katie's first communion and Sam's first T-ball game, and he has always missed Easter, Sam and Katie's birthdays, and his own birthday. "Every once in a while, Sam will just put his face in his hands and cry," Loretta says. He is six, his sister is eight, and only time will help them understand the nomadic life into which they were born.

While the Morman kids are at it, they would do well to appreciate the strength of a mother who stands a foot shorter than her husband. Loretta had to contend with Katie as a two-year-old in the foreign environs of Nashville – "I never saw the city, I was always tired" – and she had to drive from Blue Springs to Edmonton with nobody for company but Sam at two and Katie at four. Staying home with the kids for months after Russ has left for his next port of call isn't that much easier than a cross-country road trip, however. Then she must balance raising them with her own job for the local school district's Parents As Teachers Program. And every day there is a phone call from Russ. "As soon as he says hi," Loretta says, "I can tell if he had any hits."

His joy is hers. The same goes for his sadness. There is never any talk about what lies beyond his life as a player, never any discussion of his becoming a manager or a coach, or maybe just going back and getting his degree. "I know that's not very farsighted," Loretta confesses. But that's the way it has been through 11 years of marriage, and that's the way it will remain as long as Russ is chasing his dream. "She's the most loving, supporting wife anybody could ever have," he says over lunch one day in Durham, his voice thick with emotion. "I don't know what I'd do if I didn't have her."

The depth of his feelings is equaled later that week as Loretta sits in their dining room in Blue Springs, her legs pulled tight against her and a cup of coffee going cold on the table. She's thinking about everything that baseball has put Russ through, and she's struggling not to let the memories overwhelm her.

"It's hard to watch," she says, her words coming slowly. "I don't know how else to describe it. I don't want people feeling sorry for Russ. He's had a great career, and he's playing the game he loves. But he does so well and he tries so hard, and sometimes he's not given a chance. It hurts him. He doesn't show it, but it does. And I just . . . I just. . . ." Her voice trails off, and then it's her turn to cry.

§ The ring came Federal Express. It was waiting in his hotel room the day Durham opened the season in Norfolk, and when he took it out of the box, he was surprised how much heft there was to it. Must have been all the diamonds. But the diamonds didn't matter as much to him as the sight of his name and number on the ring: RUSS MORMAN 45. A lot of good men played this game for years, played it with love and honor, and rode into the sunset without a prize like the one the momentarily regal Florida Marlins gave him. All he had done for them was come up at the end of last year's pennant race, tip his cap after hitting a home run in the first game he started, and then head for Blue Springs to watch them win the World Series on TV. But he still got a ring, and when he talks about it now, he always says, "I'm lucky to have one."

No sarcasm, no bitterness, nothing except sincere gratitude – and there you have the essence of the man. Somehow he has endured into his 16th season in baseball's hinterlands without succumbing to the ugliness that we have come to take for granted among athletes making seven-digit salaries. He is the kind of ballplayer everybody in the stands always says they would be, a ballplayer who thanks his Maker that this is how he can earn a living.

The proof lies in more than the gaudy numbers Morman has in Triple A or even the workmanlike way he has gone about ringing them up. There is the wise counsel he offers young teammates, just as Carlton Fisk and George Brett offered it to him when he was the one with the bright future. And there is the simple courtesy he shows the Famous Chicken by asking, "Hey, Teddy, are we doing anything tonight?" – because he knows that Ted Giannoulas can't make his routines as the Chicken fly without volunteers. There are all those things done so frequently for so long that even the flinty characters the game prides itself on breeding can't help being moved by the man.

Sal Rende, his manager for six seasons in four towns, will tell you he loves Russ Morman like a brother – "and I'm not afraid to say it." Neither are John Boles and Smokey Garrett, who go all the way back to the beginning with him. "Without a doubt, he is as good a guy as I've ever been around in baseball," says Tampa Bay Devil Rays manager Larry Rothschild. If Rothschild didn't feel that way before this spring, he did after he handed Morman his ticket to Durham.

Morman never really had a chance to make the expansion Devil Rays, who had Fred McGriff and Paul Sorrento, two established thumpers, ahead of him at first base, and yet he had gone out and hit

.450 in the Grapefruit League. He had earned the right to gripe. But when he saw Rothschild walking toward him during batting practice, Morman broke the tension by cowering like the next victim in a slasher movie and shouting, "Stay away!"

Then he grinned and asked if he could stick around while the Devil Rays finished the spring by making their debut at Tropicana Field. With his usual devotion to duty, Morman wanted to get a feel for it in case Tampa Bay called him up. He got more than he bargained for when he hit the Trop's first home run. It didn't win him a reprieve, though, and because it came in an exhibition game, it won't be remembered by anybody except devotees of the most obscure trivia. But for the next 2 1/2 months, there must have been nights when Moran wondered if it was the last homer he would ever hit.

It wasn't until June 12 that he finally clouted his first one for the Durham Bulls. Number two came four days later, but it was still a far cry from last year in Charlotte, when he had 25 by July. This year, as he struggles to keep his batting average above .250, he finds himself racked by frustration and its cousin, confusion. "It's the hardest season I've had since I broke into A ball," he says. "All I can do is try hitting myself out of whatever is going on." So he has taken extra batting practice and studied videotape, tinkered with his stance and even changed his uniform number to lucky 45. He spent more time on the phone with Loretta, too, until she and the kids arrived in the middle of the month. "Well, yeah," he says, laughing gently at himself. "She's my psychiatrist."

No self-pity, no complaints about lingering Crash Davis comparisons, nothing except an honest desire to do right by baseball – and that also is the essence of the man. It is an unforgiving game he plays, and yet he has never let it rob him of his dreams. But don't dismiss him as a dreamer and nothing more. Why, there was a day when Russ Morman owned the whole South Side of Chicago.

Sports Illustrated, June 29, 1998

12

Bailey's Boys

The baseballs were hand-me-downs from the local semipro team, scuffed and sometimes lopsided, their seams torn so the leather flapped like the tongue on one of those dogs that were always slobbering happily at Bailey Santistevan's side. For as long as he coached – and he coached until he became a small town legend – Santistevan never had the luxury of throwing away even the most woebegone ball. Instead, he picked up needle and thread and painstakingly sewed each ragged treasure back together until it was ready for the miners' sons who could count on little other than a game in the frying pan heat of a Utah summer.

They lived in Bingham Canyon, 28 miles southwest of, and a world away from, Salt Lake City. Their fathers dug for the source of other men's riches – silver, gold, lead, and, most plentiful of all, copper – but the boys knew this canyon in the Oquirrh Mountains mainly for what it lacked. There were no lawns they could mow to earn the price of a bike and no level ground where they could ride bikes if they actually got them. There was only the old orange school bus that wheezed up Main Street on summer mornings at eight and carried them to the field where Santistevan waited with the baseballs that defined a place and an era and him.

All three are permanently intertwined in the memories of the old-timers from Bingham who will gather on the last Fourth of July of this century, just as they have on more Fourths than anybody can remember. They will turn out, as they always do, at the annual pancake breakfast in a leafy park at the canyon's mouth and breathe life back into a town officially out of existence since 1971. They will talk about the avalanches that leveled houses. And the daily 3 p.m. blasting in the world's largest open-pit copper mine. And the games that were so vital to the town that even the mine would shut down early for them. Every conversation will hum with a sense of community as indomitable as Bailey Santistevan himself. Yes, his name will come up again and again, rising out of an ethnic stew that proves what a melting pot the canyon was in a state otherwise so blond and blue-eyed that it seemed like a Viking breeding ground.

Santistevan's teams left their mark on the town, and Santistevan left his mark on the kids who played for him, whether it was at Bingham High or in his summer school of baseball. He wasn't loved by all, and he may have been hated by some, but in the end he was too big a force for anyone to ignore. "Bailey wasn't going to be your buddy," says Jimmy Brown, who cherishes the memory of every ground ball Santistevan hit to him at second base 55 years ago. "What Bailey did was influence your life. He taught us that when you play the game, you play it only one way: hard."

Santistevan expected a level of effort that had rewards far beyond the high school championships his Bingham Miners kept bringing back to the canyon. The players he coached from 1928 to '54 learned what it took to survive in a world that would hand them nothing, and the people who watched them play never forgot their passion or their swagger.

Don Gust didn't realize just what an impression those Bingham teams had made until a stranger approached him in 1970 and asked, "Aren't you that little fart who used to play for Bailey Santistevan?" Well, yes, Gust was, but *little* hardly described him anymore. He was working on the potbelly that has since become a front porch, and, more to the point, he was a grown man, an ex–minor leaguer with a wife, four sons, and a job as a high school baseball coach. And here was this stranger who remembered him from an American Legion tournament in 1946, the one over in Colorado Springs in which Gust, at 14, had been the youngest player and the hottest hitter. Admiring fans had thrust handfuls of cash at him – and Santistevan had made the kid give back every penny.

The stranger knew all about it because he had coached one of the opposing teams. Now he was a scout for the Cincinnati Reds, and he wanted Gust to work for him part time. Gust took the job, and he's still at it, working himself into a lather at tryout camps and proudly flashing his ring from the Reds' 1990 world championship. But hardly a day passes that he doesn't remember how it all started with those baseballs that anybody other than Santistevan would have thrown away. Those balls made Gust, always and forever, one of Bailey's boys.

§ Before anybody in Bingham heard of Little League, there was the Eskimo Pie League. Surely no more appealing, evocative name ever existed for anything involving boys and baseball. Santistevan concocted it in the early 1930s without corporate benediction and, so far as his old players can recall, without giving anybody an ice cream bar. All he wanted was something that would lure the boys onto the diamond when they turned six. They could keep playing in his summer program until they were 16, but the older they got, the more mundane the names of their leagues became: Pee-Wee, Middle, Giant, Major. Only once in a lifetime could a sister look at her big brother and think of him as an Eskimo Pie.

Mornings began with Bailey's boys rallying 'round the flagpole where Joe Timothy, the one-legged bus driver, deposited them. That was the way it was done at the all-dirt diamond called the Brickyard, where Santistevan's troops first played, and at the high school field that became their home in 1939. One of the players would blow *To the Colors* on a dented trumpet (Gust and his big brother, Russ, were among those who did the honors), and as soon as Old Glory was flying high, Santistevan would hand out equipment. Each game got one ball, one bat, one set of catcher's gear, and one set of bases, all well worn by the semipros who had passed them along. The result looked like something Norman Rockwell might have painted.

"You'd see young catchers, and their belly protectors would be dragging on the ground," Don Gust remembers. "And the bats, why, they'd been broken, and Bailey had nailed 'em back together and taped 'em up. They were 34 or 35 inches long, so you had to choke up on 'em, but you'd better be careful you didn't choke up so far that you hit yourself in the stomach when you swung."

For all its apparent comedy, the scene was rich in passion, the kind that made southpaw Billy Boren forget that his family was so cash strapped, he had to play with his right-handed brother's mitt. The kids chose teams from their ethnic enclaves, made out their own lineups, and hustled local businessmen for uniforms, if you call a cap bearing a sponsor's name a uniform. "The place you wanted," Gust says, "was the Elba Ruth Shop – you'd call it a boutique today. It gave you a cap and a T-shirt." Even the local brothel was good for a donation, but Daryl "Sonny" Robertson, whose nine games with the 1962 Chicago Cubs made him the only big leaguer Bingham ever produced, points out that the team sponsored by an amiable madam discreetly called itself the Main Street Boys. "Up in that town," he says with a sly smile, "*everybody* pitched in."

Bailey's boys played three hours each morning as though they had a moral obligation to repay the community with pure ferocity. Every game was a donnybrook, and if the squirts in the Eskimo Pie League rang up less than 40 runs, it was a bigger surprise than Utah voting Democrat. There were always arguments and sometimes fisticuffs, and, yes, you might say that letting the kids umpire their own games contributed to the combative atmosphere. A player from the team at bat stood behind the pitcher and called balls, strikes, and the bases. In turn, the opposition called him everything it could think of.

When the hostilities raged out of control, Santistevan would come running. "You kids quit your damn arguing!" he'd roar. "I saw that last play – and the runner was safe!" It didn't matter if Santistevan had seen the play. This was a world of his making, and he was its ultimate arbiter.

He was also the only adult allowed anywhere near the field on all but one day every summer. The exception was Parents' Day, when the mothers and fathers of Bingham were invited to watch their sons wage war on the diamond. But they had to do it on

Santistevan's terms, which meant no interfering in any way. Half a century ago, Santistevan knew what parents today have forgotten. He knew that games belong to the kids.

Nary a word of protest could be heard from those hard-bitten miners who were fathers and who saw Santistevan – or Santistevens, as some still say it – devoting his life to their sons. If he was grooming talent for himself in the process, if he was building the foundation for the nine state high school championships and five American Legion titles his teams won, well, so be it. For he was showing his players a way they might make a buck at something that had nothing to do with mining, maybe by picking up $5 or $10 a game in the state's Industrial League, maybe even by going pro. And something else: Santistevan was delivering a lesson about what it meant to be from Bingham.

"We learned how to scrap, simple as that," Jimmy Brown says. "There wasn't a white-collar kid in that canyon – it was all blue-collar. And Bailey taught us to dig down and fight for everything, because that's the way it was going to be all our lives."

§ Everybody who played for Santistevan and got hit by a pitch knew what he would hear if he was still standing: "Rub some dirt on it!" Santistevan shouted the same prescription for every bump and bruise that wasn't fatal. This was a man who knew from personal experience what it was to have a fastball dent his skull in the dark ages before batting helmets. It happened on his wedding day, an inappropriate time to be crowding the plate, much less getting hauled off to the hospital. But that was Santistevan for you, living by a code that defied all logic but his own.

He was a railroad man's son out of Jack Dempsey country in southern Colorado, born and raised in a flyspeck of a town called Los Animas, and the Utah Copper Company brought him to Bingham in 1926 to play second base. He got a job in the mine, too, which offered more security than wandering from one minor league outpost to another, the way he'd been doing since he graduated from

Colorado A&M that spring. The mine wasn't his true calling, though. Neither was second base, as it turned out.

Destiny beckoned two years later, when the principal at Bingham High School asked if Santistevan was interested in coaching. No sooner did he say yes than he had two teams to call his own, baseball and football. He never made a secret of which was his favorite sport, but he never gave football short shrift, either. He finagled his way into Knute Rockne's coaching clinics at Utah State, and he made an annual ritual of lining up his team's helmets in front of the school and painting them himself. By the time his 26-year career at Bingham had run its course, he had coached four state football champions and fathered a daughter whose name was inspired by his favorite trick play, the Susie Q.

But just looking at Santistevan staring at you out of an old newspaper photograph, you know that this was a man who thought most tricks were beneath his dignity. There's a maximum-security aspect to the grim set of his mouth, and what's left of his hair is cut short, as if he wished he didn't have to bother with it at all. Then there are his eyes. "Black, *black* eyes," says his first-born daughter, Nanette Santistevan Noble. They were a gift from his ancestors in Spain, and they became a weapon that made him seem far bigger than 5-foot-8 and 160 pounds. Even when you meet his gaze at the remove of time, they bore through you, bearing witness to all the stories you have heard about the hard line he laid down.

His players didn't drink water during practices or games, and they didn't wave at their friends in the stands. They didn't stay out past 10, and they didn't go to dances, because dances could lead to the kind of scoring their coach considered a distraction. "My dad kicked his two best players off the football team one year because they'd gone to a dance at another school," Bailey Santistevan Jr. says. "Rules were rules, even if it cost him the championship." And it did.

The father was tougher still on his only son, the strapping kid who became an entomologist and now, at 71, lives in retirement in Murrieta, California. Bailey Sr. booted Bailey Jr. square in the butt for not wearing socks in football practice, made him play fullback with a dislocated shoulder, and pulled him from a baseball game in which it looked like he would strike out every batter. Their relationship finally boiled over when Bailey Jr. heard his father say no to the New York Yankee scout who wanted to sign the boy in 1945.

"My dad wouldn't even look at the contract," Bailey Jr. recalls. "He just said, 'This boy's going to college.' Well, I got upset and joined the Marine Corps. I taught him a lesson." The sad expression on Bailey Jr.'s face as he tells the story says it was no lesson at all. His sister Nanette, a retired educator back in Salt Lake Valley, finds the words to go with the memory: "It broke my father's heart."

Bailey Santistevan the elder really did have a heart, no matter how hard he drove his son and every other son of the canyon. His heart was on display every time he sat down to mend a torn ball or a broken bat, but it didn't stop at that. There were the letters he wrote faithfully to the Bingham boys fighting World War II, and the balls he gave to kids from all over, and the 50-cent pieces Bailey Jr. once saw him press into the hands of two scared, penniless, not-so-tough guys fresh from Salt Lake's juvenile detention center. "He never spanked his own kids, either," Nanette says. "My mother did."

What's more, Santistevan had some very public moments of vulnerability, usually when he got so wrapped up in coaching that he forgot about his diabetes and went into insulin shock. "He'd start acting like he was drunk," Don Gust says. "It scared the hell out of you the first time you saw it happen." But after that, his players knew what to do. They would race to his duplex next to the school, where his wife, Edith, always kept a pitcher of orange juice laced with sugar. As soon as he got that in him, Santistevan would be back to normal. Normal by his standards, that is.

So let's assume his insulin level was where it belonged that day in 1950 when Bingham was down two runs in the state championship baseball game and Gust was coming to bat with the bases loaded. Here was the perfect man for the situation: the Miners' cleanup hitter, a slugging shortstop who would go on to sign with the Detroit Tigers for $3,000 when that was a fat bonus. But Santistevan called

Gust over for a confab, and the first thing he told his star was, "I don't think you want to hit today."

"Yes, I do," Gust said.

"No," Santistevan said, "I better get somebody out there who wants to hit."

"But I *want* to hit," Gust said.

On and on they went, until Gust was so cross-eyed with rage that he was ready to chew his bat down to a toothpick. Then Santistevan walked away, and Gust hit the triple that proved they had both done their jobs.

§ By now you shouldn't need to be told who used to say that the winners walk on Main Street and the losers walk in the alleys. The credo exerted more than a little pressure on Bailey's boys for the simple reason that the only street in the canyon was Main Street. It snaked for three miles, from the French enclave called Frogtown at the bottom to the copper mine at the top. Main was scarcely more than 20 feet at its widest, just enough for two cars to squeeze past each other, and it was always fodder for the wits who insisted that dogs in the canyon had to wag their tails up and down.

As for alleys, there were none. Instead there were the gullies and ravines where people settled even before the population peaked at 15,000 in 1930, making living space on the only paved street as tight as a pair of secondhand shoes. Residents gravitated toward their own kind, in places with names no suburb could ever have: Greeks in Greek Camp, Scandinavians in Carr Fork, Slavs in Highland Boy, and so on. But when you hear that Bingham High's class of 1950 counted 18 nationalities among its 55 graduates, you know there was no way all those ethnic groups could have avoided each other. Squeezed together, they came to realize they were bound by their blue collars. Their hunger fueled the fire that Santistevan lit in his ballplayers.

"People in Salt Lake Valley acted like they were afraid of us," says Billy Boren, a star tailback and center fielder from Bingham's class of '47 who grew up to become a prominent businessman and a

Mormon bishop. "We were from the other side of the tracks, so they got it in their mind that we were almost gangsters."

What they were, really, was poor kids whose parents rented houses for $10 a month or bought them for $500. Kids who knew what it was to use a dynamite box from the Hercules Company as a chair. Kids who, even in winter, slept on porches with only a sheet between them and the elements. Kids who watched their fathers sign their paychecks over to the Bingham Mercantile, knowing they would have to go to a clerk in that many splendored store if they wanted so much as a dime for the movies. Kids who never heard their fathers plot to escape to a better life. "All they talked about," says Jimmy Brown, who grew up to know success in sporting goods and graphic design, "was being a track boss or a timekeeper. It was never a doctor or a lawyer. They were blue collar, and they never thought they could be anything else."

The promise of honest work brought them to this wedge of the Oquirrhs, discovered in 1848 by two young Mormon settlers – the Bingham brothers, Thomas and Sanford – and dominated first by the Utah Copper Company and then Kennecott Copper. The fathers of Santistevan's ballplayers were paid wages, often no more than a dollar an hour, that kept them on a short leash and made them thankful for small favors. "I remember when we got a raise to $1.02," says Gust, who worked his way through the University of Utah on the night shift. "I thought I was rich."

He was, but in ways that had nothing to do with the almighty dollar, ways that he wouldn't realize until he was older and Bingham was no more. Then he, like so many of Bailey's boys, would look back and remember how Santistevan brought the town together with his teams, giving people a rooting interest in something far more valuable than copper: their sons.

Bingham became a place where American Legion baseball games that would have drawn 20 parents and friends in Salt Lake City were good for throngs of 700. Come the high school football season, the field would be ringed two and three deep with fans who arrived early to avoid the crush in the bleachers. The Pastime Saloon ran a pool on every game that a Bingham team played, no matter what the sport. When the Miners finally won a state basketball championship, in 1960, the shopkeepers threw open their doors for a bash to end them all. "The dads were offering to get the Mormon kids drinks," says George Sluga, the former Eskimo Pie Leaguer who led the champs in scoring and has since coached Bingham to six more titles. "I think everybody was happy because they'd won so much money betting on us."

To look at the old high school today, it's hard to believe it could ever have housed the white-hot passion that Santistevan ignited. The two-story brick edifice sits abandoned and forlorn, its name now adorning a modern structure in nearby West Jordan, in the thick of the upscale swirl that consumes Salt Lake Valley.

Behind that padlocked relic is an even sadder sight: the mammoth field that the Miners used as a diamond and a gridiron and that Santistevan held claim to every summer by running 10 or 12 kids' baseball games at once. Time and weather have joined forces to split home plate down the middle. The infield is so overgrown that you can barely make it out. The concrete football bleachers in rightfield are spider-webbed with cracks, and the wooden baseball grandstand has vanished.

But on the Fourth of July last year, if you talked to the men who played there as Bailey's boys, you came away believing that this ragged wasteland is an illusion and that the men's memories are the reality. They gathered beneath the cottonwood trees in Copperton Park, and they ate the pancakes that the Lions Club and the Volunteer Fire Department served up, and they remembered everything as clearly as if the Eskimo Pie League were only yesterday.

There was Kent Stillman, retired from the navy, remembering how he used to play for Santistevan all day, then rush off at twilight to hang numbers on the scoreboard at the semipro games. There was Sonny Robertson, retired from the Salt Lake County Sheriff's Department, remembering how he drove his coach nuts by trying to hit home runs over a left-field fence that was 400 feet away. (Of course, Santistevan always got even at the next practice by hitting

Sonny 100 extra grounders.) And there was Gust, remembering the big brother who was among the first of Bailey's boys.

Russell Gust, 10 years Don's senior, lived his life as if Santistevan had charted it: Went off to college in Ohio and had John Glenn for a classmate. Played minor league ball even though he had mangled his throwing hand in his father's printing press when he was a kid. Earned a handsome living as a chemist in Nevada. And made sure his kid brother had a baseball mitt, so he too could be one of Bailey's boys and play the game that ruled the canyon.

"Russ died in '94," Don said. "Heart just blew out on him." But no sooner had the words left his mouth than Don realized they were an insufficient tribute to a man who lived to be 72 and always abided by the lessons that Santistevan taught him. "I'll tell you something, though," Don added quickly. "He played golf right up to the end on nothing but medication." There it was, proof that Russ had stayed the course that began in the Eskimo Pie League. Only one thing was allowed to stop him.

§ They still talk about Tommy Pazell as one of Bailey's boys who could have made it, but when he graduated with the class of '37, he looked like a better fit for someone's pocket than for the big leagues. Stood 5-foot-3, weighed 104 pounds, and here was the kicker: He was barely 15. But Santistevan never did the easy thing by writing him off as a shrimp. "He was real fair, just like a coach should be," Pazell says all these years later. "If you tried, you played." And when Pazell played, whether he was lashing a base hit or chasing down a fly ball, he got bigger and bigger, until he simply couldn't be ignored.

The fight to be noticed was force of habit with Tommy by then. He had started kindergarten a year early because he didn't want his four older brothers leaving him at home, and he had skipped the sixth grade because he was as smart as he was small. Never did he let his size beat him. He learned the virtue of resourcefulness from his father, who kept whistles wet in bone-dry Utah by bootlegging wine. "I stomped on so many grapes," Tommy likes to joke, "that they called me Purple Toes Pazell." But every laugh he found in Bingham seemed to be offset by a lesson in life's hard edge. Why, at age five, he saw two men killed because of mindless ethnic hatred.

Suffice it to say, his illusions w 're few when he became one of Bailey's boys. Maybe that amplified all the good experiences that lay ahead of him. Santistevan told Pazell he would play if he busted his butt, and each held up his part of the bargain. Santistevan also said Pazell might make some extra money playing semipro ball after he graduated, and that proved true as well. Pazell made $6 a day swinging a maul in the copper mine and $6 for every game he was in center field for Gemmell Club, the local semipro team. He did that for four years, saving what he didn't hand over to his mother and growing six inches and gaining 46 pounds. He still wasn't a monster, but he was big enough for a Boston Red Sox scout to notice him.

"Kid got any power?" the scout asked Santistevan. As if on cue, Pazell smote a home run. "Yeah, but can he run?" the scout asked. Next time up, Pazell beat out a bunt for a single. And that was how the Red Sox came to sign him, which was more than even Santistevan had ever promised.

Pazell headed for Canton, Ohio, in the Class C Mid-Atlantic League, with the glove he had paid for by shoveling snow, and, as he puts it, "I did good." It's right there in his scrapbook: the .293 batting average, the 17 stolen bases. He went to Double A Scranton near the end of that season and could have stayed on the next. Problem was, it was 1942.

World War II was getting uglier by the minute and Bailey's boys were tripping over each other in their eagerness to fight the Axis powers. Pazell wasn't about to be left behind. He ended up in Patton's Third Army as a tech sergeant who got a battlefield promotion to second lieutenant. "It wasn't because of bravery," he says. "I just knew what I was doing." His specialty was artillery. So there he was, in France, lobbing howitzer shells at the Germans, when they answered in kind. The shrapnel from the blast knocked Pazell's left knee out from under him and sent his baseball career to an early grave.

He could have had it worse, of course. He could have been one of the 15 sons of Bingham who died in the Good War. He could have been as dead as Ernie Sheen, the good-natured galoot who hit so many homers for Santistevan that the whole town thought he was the next Babe Ruth. But Pazell lived, and so he had to face what he would never be. He would never be a big leaguer.

The bitterness of that disappointment could have eaten at him for the rest of his days. But that wasn't how Bailey's boys were taught to get along. They were taught to pick themselves up and move on as best they could, which is why Pazell would spend 29 years as a teacher and vice principal at Bingham High. He wasn't just doing what Santistevan taught him. He was doing what Santistevan did. It was a good life.

§ The canyon stands behind a gate now, off limits to the unauthorized. If you want to see where the town of Bingham used to be, you have to drive four miles south and follow a new road up to the visitors' center at the copper mine. It's not a trip that many of the old-timers take. You could understand why when you saw Don Gust peer hopefully over the rim of the canyon for the first time in maybe a decade, then pull back with a stunned look.

"They filled in the whole damn thing," he said, his voice little more than a whisper. For a long moment he was silent, and silence is rare for this live wire with laughing blue eyes. But nothing could have prepared Gust for the sight of his boyhood home buried beneath the tons of earth that have been moved as the mine has expanded. "They always told us it would happen," he said finally, "but holy cow. . . ."

His whole world had shifted, and no matter what age and experience had taught him, he didn't want to accept it any more than he wanted to remember the way the town looked at the end, with only 1,500 residents hanging on. He wanted there to be something about Bingham that endured, something that would carry its memory into the next century and remind people that such places once gave the nation its foundation and its backbone. Hearing Gust talk about Bailey Santistevan, you can't help thinking of the coach as the perfect champion of that long-gone canyon's glory. For one thing, a lot of the glory was of his making. For another, he seemed too tough to cave in to anything as ephemeral as time.

But the truth arrived on a June day in 1954, when Santistevan was just back from fishing in Mexico with the son who had turned from adversary to buddy. He had been out in the garden, and then he had walked into the house. "My mother saw him go inside," says Nanette. "When she went in a little later, he was dead." His heart had stopped him at 53, worn out from the battle with diabetes.

Santistevan lay in state in the teachers' lounge at the high school, and the crowd lined up for blocks to pay its last respects. Then so many people filed into the auditorium for the funeral service that there weren't any seats left. Those who couldn't find one had to gather on the front lawn. When there was no more room on the lawn, they spilled into the street.

Of all the people who turned out that day, the first to come to Nanette's mind is one of those sweet, sad souls every small town seems to have. His name was Reggie, and he shook a lot and stuttered, and he loved Bingham's teams more than the mountain air he breathed. He never missed a game, home or away, and sometimes when Reggie would be out hitchhiking to keep his streak intact, Santistevan would stop the team bus and give him a ride. Now Reggie had come to repay the kindness. "He knew my father always carried hard candy for his diabetes," Nanette says, "so that's what he brought to the funeral service. He wanted us to put it in his pocket before they closed the casket."

Reggie got his wish. And the story became a treasure worthy of telling in the century ahead. Pass it on.

Sports Illustrated, July 5, 1999

Source Acknowledgments

"Of Stars and Angels," *Sports Illustrated*, June 21, 1993.

"Laughing on the Outside," *Sports Illustrated*, June 26, 2000.

"The Right-hander," originally published as "Touching Base with a Dream," *Chicago Sun-Times*, December 31, 1980.

"Out in the Cold," originally published as "Midsummer's Night Dreamer Left Out in Cold," *Chicago Sun-Times*, February 11, 1981.

"Fathers and Sons," originally published as "Hey, Dads, Make Baseball Fun for Your Sons," *Chicago Sun-Times*, June 20, 1982.

"Baseball without Justice," *Chicago Sun-Times*, March 9, 1980.

" . . . And Checking It Twice," originally published as "Bill Veeck Making List, Checking It Twice," *Chicago Daily News*, December 16, 1977.

"Prelude to Goodbye," originally published as "Of Sir Bill, a Knight Valorous, Beguiling" *Chicago Sun-Times*, September 28, 1980.

"Selling the Sox," originally published as "Selling the Sox Warms Veeck – to a Degree," *Chicago Sun-Times*, February 4, 1981.

"To the Bleachers Once More," originally published as "Hit of the Bleachers Is No Bum," *Chicago Sun-Times*, July 25, 1982.

"Twilight of the Long-ball Gods," *Inside Sports*, August 31, 1981.

"The Wild, Wild Past," originally published as "Tom Brookshier's Wild, Wild Past," *Philadelphia Magazine*, September 1994.

"Beginner's Luck," originally published as "Just Beginner's Luck," *Chicago Sun-Times*, September 5, 1980.

"The Buddy System," originally published as "It's Not Indecent to Say, 'I'll Miss You,'" *Chicago Daily News*, June 17, 1977.

"The Big Man Steps Up," originally published as "Nothing beneath Towering Dignity of Mets' Generous Giant," *Chicago Sun-Times*, August 7, 1983.

"A Little House That Built Ruth," *Chicago Sun-Times*, July 10, 1981.

"Marilyn and Joe," originally published as "A Love That Redeems All Enhanced Marilyn and Joe," *Chicago Sun-Times*, December 25, 1983.

"The Clown," originally published as "Patkin Still Leaves Them Laughing," *Philadelphia Daily News*, May 7, 1985.

"Rocky's Road," originally published as "On Tobacco Road," *Chicago Sun-Times*, June 2, 1980.

"Last Licks," originally published as "McCarver Finds Last Licks Have a Special Flavor," *Chicago Sun-Times*, September 21, 1980.

"These Bees Are Bad News," *Philadelphia Daily News*, April 29, 1986.

"Beautiful Dreamers," *GQ*, April 1996.

"K48," originally published as "Middle-aged Crazy, or Is He Simply Batty?" *Chicago Sun-Times*, February 24, 1982.

"American Legion Summers," originally published as "The Joys of Legion Ball Aren't Foreign to Him," *National Sports Daily*, August 24, 1990.

"Basil,"*Sporting News*, October 25, 1980.

"Hilly and Garvey," originally published as "His Beloved Dodgers Never Let Him Down," *Chicago Sun-Times*, May 28, 1982.

"Baseball Blues," *Chicago Sun-Times*, November 5, 1982.

"A Mischievous Eye on Time," *Chicago Sun-Times*, July 2, 1980.

"Wild Bill," originally published as "Wild Bill Hagy: An Oriole Fan Who's Larger Than Life," *Chicago Sun-Times*, October 16, 1979.

"On the Road to Sioux Falls," originally published as "The Best Game Imaginable," *Philadelphia Daily News*, April 15, 1986.

"Morman's Mission," *Sports Illustrated*, June 29, 1998.

"Bailey's Boys," *Sports Illustrated*, July 5, 1999.

About the Author

John Schulian has ventured from newspapers and magazines to Hollywood and back again. He worked as a sports columnist in Chicago and Philadelphia, was one of the creators of TV's *Xena: Warrior Princess*, and remains a special contributor to *Sports Illustrated*. His prose has been included in *The Best American Sports Writing* and *SI's Fifty Years of Great Writing*. He was a sports commentator for National Public Radio and has written about sports and popular culture for *GQ*, the *New York Times*, the *Los Angeles Times*, the *Oxford American*, and msnbc.com. Among his television writing and producing credits are *Miami Vice, Wiseguy, The "Slap" Maxwell Story, Midnight Caller, Hercules: The Legendary Journeys*, and *JAG*. He is the author of *Writers' Fighters and Other Sweet Scientists*, a collection of his boxing journalism. He lives in Pasadena, California.